Pastoral in Palestine

Neil Hertz

PRICKLY PARADIGM PRESS
CHICAGO

Prickly Paradigm Press, LLC
5629 South University Avenue
Chicago, Il 60637

www.prickly-paradigm.com

ISBN: 978-0984-20103-7
LCCN: 2012948395

Printed in the United States of America on acid-free paper.

During the late winter and spring of 2011, I was living in Ramallah and teaching just outside East Jerusalem, at the Abu Dis campus of Al-Quds University, in a collaborative program set up by the University and Bard College. The reports collected here were initially sent back to some friends curious to learn what life was like in the Occupied Territories of the West Bank. My experience of that life was limited. Without Arabic, I could converse only with those Palestinians who spoke English. I was not allowed to visit the horrors of Gaza, nor did I spend time in the refugee camps or the villages, where the burdens of the Occupation are considerably more oppressive than they are in Ramallah itself or at my university. Nevertheless, I got to see and hear a good deal; I leave the judgment of the pertinence of these accounts to my reader.

12 January 2011: water tanks

I first noticed the water tanks on top of Palestinian houses several summers ago—the beat-up old metal tanks in places like the Deheisha refugee camp outside Bethlehem contrasted with the spiffier black tanks on the roofs of newer construction in Ramallah. This time, driving over to Ramallah from Ben Gurion Airport, the line  between Israel proper and the Occupied Territories was marked by the contrast, in the towns we passed, between Israeli buildings with no water tanks visible and those—across the frontier—with multiple tanks, corresponding to the number of apartments in the building. Why? Because Israeli buildings receive continuous water supply, whereas supply on the West Bank is controlled by the Israeli-owned water provider and is not guaranteed; sometimes it's only available 50% of the time, I was told.

Hence the need for storage tanks. A striking welcome to this land of finely tuned discriminations.

15 January: short cuts, misprisions

Heading from Ramallah to West Jerusalem, the taxi driver, a Palestinian in his 60's working for an East Jerusalem outfit, takes an unpaved back road to avoid the famously unpredictable Qalandia checkpoint. Back in October I had been stuck in a huge traffic jam, several hundred cars, on the wrong side of that checkpoint for about an hour and finally got off the bus and walked the half-mile or so back into Ramallah. But of course the back road I'm on this time is not some secret Palestinian tunnel: everyone, including the young IDF soldiers manning the Qalandia checkpoint, knows about it. So what then's the point of the checkpoint, if "terrorists" can always come into West Jerusalem this way?

It's 6 in the evening and dark outside. The driver had been talking real estate on our way out of Ramallah—who can build, how much licenses cost, why

so much construction is half-finished—and pointing out buildings where, along the roadside, the shops are lit but where there are no lights—no tenants, sometimes no walls—in the apartments above. Now we're beyond those shops and out in a darkened semi-rural area; he tells me that where I see clusters of bluish-white street lights on the slopes, those are Arab villages, but that the orange-yellow lights (often higher up the hillsides) indicate Jewish settlements. That seems clear enough until, a little farther along, he gestures towards some bluish-white lights and says that they're from a settlement, too. So is the rule of thumb not a rule of thumb? I've been here four days and already it's clear that in conversations with both Palestinians and Israelis what people assert with confidence often is less than reliable.

Take those water tanks. I asked one Ramallan what the newer, black ones were made of. He said rubber on the outside and metal within (as opposed to the older ones that were just metal). And went on to explain that the older ones were vulnerable to being punctured by Israeli bullets, and that the rubber somehow acted as a seal when the bullet went through. But in the village of Bir Zeit yesterday, a Palestinian artist who is rehabbing an old house as a cultural center and had just installed some of the black rubber tanks said that no, there was no metal inside them—they were just rubber, and if punctured would leak. (In fact, I  later learned, they're not rubber but plastic.) And, to further complicate things, when I finally got to West Jerusalem the other evening, via that back road, guests at dinner corrected me: one could indeed find black water tanks in Israel (although more often they were white) where they are hooked up to solar panels as storage units for heated water; these Jerusalemites agreed, however, that the tanks' function in the West Bank was, as I had been told, to store water against Israeli cut-offs of the supply. My point is not that these questions can't be settled with a little patient research, but rather that all these potential matters of fact are surrounded, in common conversations on both sides of the frontier, by a haze of half-baked understandings and misprisions. If you want to get this country, these countries, wrong, it helps, like me, not to speak either Hebrew or Arabic.

But it also helps just to be living here, on one side of the border or the other.

I'm attaching some Ramallah photos: one is of the building where I've rented a 5th-floor apartment on

a street that is about 200 yards long but has a name: Salvador Allende Street (a quarter-mile downhill from Edward Said Street). The other is of the wall of a building across the way, a nice example of the older vernacular Arab architecture.

21 January: the ride to Abu Dis

The minibus ride from Ramallah—where many of the Americans teaching in the Bard/Al-Quds program live—to the University's campus, in Abu Dis, a village a couple of miles east of the Old City of Jerusalem, usually takes almost an hour. As the crow flies, it's about 11 miles, maybe less, but the trip is lengthened partly by the dramatic topography of the hills to be negotiated, partly by the necessity of taking a route that stays outside the Wall separating East Jerusalem from the West Bank. Here's a shot of one section of the Wall visible from the campus looking west toward Jerusalem. The original siting of the Wall would have had it cutting right through the campus; that was modified at the request of the University, but its path still cuts off the school from some contiguous neighborhoods of Abu Dis where many of the students live. To get to their classes they have to take a

long way around. [To learn more about the Wall, or about the Israeli state's other bizarre inventions for controlling Palestinian space, read René Bachmann's *A Wall in Palestine* and Eyal Weizman's *Hollow Land*].

Riding over to campus the other day, I was sitting next to an Al-Quds epidemiologist, a Palestinian in his thirties who'd studied in London, then spent five years in Berlin; an expert on a particularly virulent parasitic disease, he had worked for the WHO on public health matters in Lucknow in India. He told me he had liked living in Berlin—it was, as he put it, "so systematic," so logical. London he had found "confusing," and as for Lucknow—forget it! By now we had left the outskirts of Ramallah behind and were passing through the beginnings of the Judean hills. Looking across his chest, out the van's window, I was absorbed by the sights along the way: the stunningly bleak desert landscape, the odd shapes of eroded limestone, the Bedouin encampments in the pockets of the hills. But for all this the epidemiologist evinced neither interest nor sympathy. I asked him about the shrubs pressing up among the rocks; he said they were typical, then went on to retell the legend—from the Koran? he wasn't sure—of how God, as a punishment for mankind's sins, had, in a sort of topological version of Noah's Flood, turned the surface of the Earth inside out, revealing these stones, so hostile to life.

That, as a matter of fact, was also Herman Melville's take on Judea and the stones of the Old City:

Whitish mildew pervading whole tracts of land-scape—bleached—leprosy—encrustation of curses—old cheese—bones of rocks—crunched, gnawed, & mumbled—mere refuse & rubble of creation—like that laying outside of Jaffa gate—All Judea seems to have been an accumulation of this rubbish—You see the anatomy—compares with ordinary regions as skeleton to a living and rosy man—So rubbishy, that no chiffonier could find anything all over it—No moss as in other ruins—no grace of decay—no ivy—the unleavened nakedness of desolation—whitish ashes—lime kilns.

Strange that the chronicler of the White Whale didn't recognize the Bleached Sublime when presented with another instance of it.

24 January: Ma'ale Adumim, pastoral rationality

I found the above photo on the web: it's taken from an angle I couldn't position myself at, and it gives a good sense of Ma'ale Adumim, one of the largest of the settlements on the West Bank, a "neighborhood" in Israeli parlance; to Palestinians, who have no stake in that particular euphemism, a "colony." It is a bedroom community of about 40,000 people just to the east of Jerusalem. I pass along the base of its hill on the way from Ramallah to Abu Dis every day. Located as it is, its effect and—we have every reason to believe—its intention, was to interrupt the contiguity of Palestinian territory on the West Bank. But its "settlers" are not zealots with Uzis; for the most part, I'm told, they're secular families looking for reasonably priced garden apartments. Jerusalem is crowded and expensive, and many secular Israelis are discouraged from living there by the increasingly felt presence of the ultra-Orthodox. The goatherd in the foreground is not an Orientalist

prop, trundled in for tourists, like the locally famous Jericho camels, but a working herdsman—we would pass dozens of them along the way to school. Still, this is what Edward Said would recognize as an Orientalist image in its ambivalent hierarchical juxtaposition of two ways of life—what William Empson would have called a "version of pastoral."

In 2002, Thomas Leitersdorf, the chief architect of Ma'ale Adumim, was asked by an interviewer, "Did the Arab villages that can be seen in the area influence your architecture?" This was his response, in full:

> I look upon the morphology of the Arab villages with envy. The beauty of the Arab village lies in its accumulative and somewhat irrational nature—development progresses slowly, with each generation adding on to the existing fabric built by its predecessor. Our approach, on the other hand, determined by the government, produces an instant city. In three years we churned out a couple of thousand apartments—all built on one concept, one system of construction and infrastructure. For them it is different. In the beginning there was a donkey track. A man builds a home, a son is born, the son gets married and they need to add something, so they add it on to the area of the street. But so long as there is still room enough for the donkey, there is no room for the car and all that it entails. But if you look at this process logically, by today's standards, you can't build a city this way. You can't pass up the necessary infrastructure or traffic and you can't provide a minimum level of services. But in terms of beauty they are way ahead of us! Architecture without architects—this is the Arab village, and this is its beauty. It is always better than when an architect comes in; the architect only

spoils things because the architect has to work logi-
cally, and they do not.

Astonishing prose. My Palestinian epidemiologist colleague might appreciate the "rationality"—it's
what he liked about Berlin—but would he buy this fable

about "them," their
donkeys and their sons?
"For them it is differ-
ent." So the story goes:
"In the beginning..."—
even before there was a
donkey track, there must
have been a donkey.
Then the donkey made
the track, the man made the home (and the son) and
before long—give or take a millennium—you have the
enviable morphology of the Arab village—somewhat
irrational, out of the question for the likes of us—we'd
"only spoil things"—but "in terms of beauty, way ahead
of us." We know what Leitersdorf means, and even what
he's drawing on. When he cites "Architecture without
architects" he's referring to a famous 1960s exhibit at
New York's Museum of Modern Art dedicated to
vernacular building practices around the world and
intended to contest the dominant high modernist
International Style. And the architect's *soi-disant* "envy"?
This is pure pastoral, and one of the reasons, when asked
by a Bard dean to offer a poetry course that had some
"conceptual or theoretical" structure to it—mere close
reading being, apparently, the pedagogical equivalent of
tracking a donkey—I thought of Empson's rich historical study, *Some Versions of Pastoral*, and decided to offer a
course entitled "The Pastoral Impulse in Poetry and

Society." I imagined that this would allow me to read a bunch of poems, but also to include works like James Agee's and Walker Evans' *Let Us Now Praise Famous Men*, works which engaged the politics of cultural difference.

Apropos politics, Leitersdorf had this to say at the close of the interview: "As to the politics of Jews and Arabs, I cannot contribute because I am very weak on politics. To tell you that an architect influences politics? He doesn't. The whole story of Judea and Samaria could have been different, but this is on levels that are neither in your hands nor mine." [The entire interview, and much more, may be found in *A Civilian Occupation: The Politics of Israeli Architecture*].

P.S. Setting all this down reminded me that, as our bus pulled into the "irrational" cluster of houses and streets that forms the village of Abu Dis, my epidemiologist seatmate (who commutes, as I do, from Ramallah) displayed the same disdain for the villagers that he had for the landscape, noting that they were a backward lot, slow to see the advantages of having a university there in town: they hadn't developed amenities for the students, there was no planning, etc. Abu Dis has no Collegetown, alas. (And indeed, that was one of the reasons I had been advised to look for an apartment elsewhere.)

25 January: Al Jazeera

A new banner in the main square reads "*Al-Jazeera* is not for the Arabs; it's for the Israelis." Ramallah is the seat of the Palestinian Authority, so it's not surprising that people here, whether prompted by their government or not, are angry about the leaks just published by *Al-Jazeera* (and *The Guardian*) suggesting considerable cooperation between the PA and Israeli government bureaus. So a crowd gathered (or was gathered) in the square this afternoon, then marched off first to the *Al-Jazeera* offices in the City Center, then to the PA HQ, to show their support for Abbas. People I talked with didn't deny the truth of the allegations of the PA's complicity with the Israelis, but questioned the timing of this bit of (much-needed, they would add) "transparency."

27 January: rubbish, rubble, rabble

Melville's use of "rubbish" for what we would call "rubble" sent me to Wikipedia, where I learned that, in the 19th century, both words were used to refer to loose rocks of different sizes lying about. Hard not to think about rubble here: it's all over the place—as scree at the base of limestone escarpments in the desert, as cement construction debris, or as rubble walls, intact, or dilapidated. The local topography, the pitch of its hillsides, the necessity of terracing for any agriculture, fields or groves, even for small urban gardens, bespeaks the gravitational pull that has to be constantly counteracted. So retaining walls become part of the ongoing work of settlement, what Thomas Leitersdorf might call the logic of modern urban planning, the "systematic" aspect my epidemiologist colleague so admired about Berlin.

In that connection, take a look at a recent work entitled "Family Parade" by the Taiwanese artist Chen Shun-chu. Carefully aligned on the walls of a roofless stone hut are 200-odd photographic portraits of individuals of all ages—Chen's family parade—seen across the top of a heap of stone building material, perhaps once part of the dilapidated structure. One's eye moves among the variously  discernible likenesses of men and women, and back and forth between the portraits and the rubble in the foreground. A ladder, overtopping the hut, offers an upward vector consonant with the organized ("rational") look of the portraits-on-parade, but the power of the work develops out of the sensed entropic pull downward—from structure to heap, from people to fragments of stone. The suggestion is that this is the destiny of order as well as one's own individual destination, what Robert Lowell has called "the downward glide and bias of existence."

A more pertinent instance of the equation of people with stones, in this case of "rabble" with "rubble," may be seen in a painting by Ernest Meissonier of the scattered remains of a Parisian barricade's paving stones and of its defenders during the June Days of the Revolution of 1848.

At a dinner party in West Jerusalem recently, two of the guests had just returned from a stay in Hamburg, where they had been struck by the ubiquitous presence of Stolpersteine, the "stumbling-blocks" inserted by the artist Gunter Demnig among the paving stones of the sidewalks in front of houses where Jews had lived before their deportation and murder in the 40's. The hostess remarked that similar stones, giving names to the faceless departed, might well be placed around Jerusalem in front of the houses of exiled Arab families. A silence fell among these Israelis, acknowledging the slim likelihood of this ever coming to pass. All were deplorers of "The Situation," one had gone to jail rather than fight in Lebanon in the 80's, the others were variously active in protesting their government's

policies. These were people for whom the Palestinians are precisely not "rabble" to be treated as "rubble." But I think some such equation must exist in the minds of many of their compatriots, where it functions to rationalize increasingly bad solutions to a political problem. Political problems are never merely practical; thinking about them is laced with the fear of death, of personal and national disintegration, and other inevitable fantasies. In this respect, one could consider the wall encompassing Ma'ale Adumim not just as a defense against "terrorists" storming the hilltop from below, but as one more retaining wall, keeping the colonists from an imaginary, uncontrolled, totally irrational descent to join the rabble as rubble and scree.

4 February: an upscale East Jerusalem neighborhood

Classes start this weekend, so yesterday I met with Omar Yousef, the Palestinian architect and planner with whom I shall be teaching a cities course, to go over our readings. Afterwards, I asked to see some of the buildings he'd designed, so he drove me around East Jerusalem, pointing them out. In an upscale neighborhood called Shu'fat we were looking at a coop apartment house considerably modified by

 the addition of a couple of stories to his earlier design, when the stylishly dressed couple who owned one of the apartments came out, at first suspicious of these people taking pictures of their place, but then interested in talking with its architect. At one point, the woman dashed back inside and emerged with a document from the Israeli authorities announcing that the building was to be demolished, and its owner had 30 days in which to appeal this decision. Lowering her voice so as not to embarrass the owner (who might be listening in his ground-floor apartment), alternately sardonically amused and bitterly angry with the Israelis, the woman explained that indeed there'd been some illegalities in the added-on construction, but that this was just the sort of bureaucratic harassment that Palestinians had become accustomed to. This was no cinder-block bricolage, but an elegant and solid, upper-middle-class building. Hard to understand what the municipality of Jerusalem or the State of Israel has to gain by its demolition. Or not so hard.

****

Some readers have asked what I thought of what's going on in Cairo. More or less what anyone in Ithaca or Baltimore or Nome, with a laptop and a TV set, may be thinking, i.e., nothing authoritative. Why, even the State Department's spokesman, P.J. Crowley, at a recent briefing claimed not to know who those violent anti-protesters were the other night! In my living room,

the TV these days is tuned to *Al-Arabiya*'s coverage of Tahrir Square. (*Al-Jazeera*, still *non grata* in Ramallah, has been zapped off the screen.) The prints on the wall, by the way, were supplied by my Palestinian landlord, who has decorated his apartments and hallways with transient Westerners in mind; they are popular reproductions of the watercolors David Roberts, the English Orientalist artist, did in the late 1830s.

11 February: a cosmopolitan evening in Ramallah

The Bir Zeit University sociologist Lisa Taraki has written of Ramallah as a prosperous bubble of cosmopolitanism within the West Bank, a place where investment capital and political power (such as it is) have accumulated as a result of the Israelis having, so far, blocked the establishment of a Palestinian political capital in East Jerusalem. (See her "Enclave Metropolis" in the *Journal of Palestine Studies*). That cosmopolitanism was on display last night, when the Palestinian-American comedian, Maysoon Zayid, came to town.

The event was held at the Friends Boys School, a complex of handsome Levantine buildings built around the time of the First World War and surrounding a small formal garden. One traversed the courtyard and entered a scene that could have taken place in Ithaca, N.Y.: middle-school boys in white shirts and dark trousers standing in rows to welcome the guests, the usual uncomfortable seats descending to a stage with a dais, from which the School's Principal, a handsome woman in a pants suit, addressed us in Arabic and English, speaking mostly of the School's history and programs. An overflow crowd, so lots of stirring until everyone could get seated, some with their suppers on their laps. The audience seemed mostly middle-class Anglophone parents with their kids—all their kids, including some toddlers. Hired babysitters, I was told, aren't much used around here; either you have a grandmother or an aunt or you take the kids with you. Then the warm-up acts came on: another Palestinian-American woman who was quite funny in her own right, and a short bouncy guy who only performed in Arabic, but who had all the moves and mike-tricks of a seasoned stand-up comic. Then Maysoon herself for two sets, one in English, the other in Arabic. She's a quick witty woman with wonderful timing and a routine that struck me as familiarly Catskill: jokes about the Arab Mother, the Heavy Father, the Dopey Girlfriend, the When-Are-You-Going-To-Meet-A-Nice-Arab-Boy-And-Get-Married-Already?-Conversation, etc., many of them brought off hilariously. In front of me two middle-aged women, one in a headscarf, were rocking back and forth with laughter, particularly at the husband-and-wife jokes. Further down the aisle sat their balding husbands, also amused, but perhaps a bit less so. There were political jokes, too, more in the Arabic set, about Islamophobia in the U.S., about being interrogated by Israelis at the Tel Aviv airport, about Erekat and the Palestinian Authority, and, of course, about Mubarak. I got whispered translations of some of them from the Bir Zeit teacher sitting next to me, who deserves a paragraph of her own in this piece on cosmopolitanism.

On my arrival in Ramallah, I got in touch with a graduate school friend of my son's, a woman teaching economics at Bir Zeit, and she, in turn, introduced me to her Arabic teacher, a philosopher and literary critic, who had an apartment—her sister's—that I might be interested in renting. I didn't take the apartment, which was stunningly located on the cusp of a ravine but in a recently developed and isolated area far from the center of town, but I did keep in touch with the philosopher, because she had just completed a dissertation (in Norwegian) on the Jerusalem poetry of Yehuda Amichai and Mahmoud Darwish, the two great contemporary poets of the Israeli/Palestinian conflict, and I was hoping to get her to talk with our students. She grew up in a village north of Ramallah, went to Bir Zeit, but went on to do her graduate work in Norway, interrupting it for a time to work with an NGO in India that was seeking to rehabilitate the young girls who had been "chosen" as temple prostitutes. She left after a few months, she said, because she "felt too white." Now she was teaching courses on the history of Western and Islamic philosophy as well as supplementing her income by teaching Arabic, as she had done while studying in Norway. Would she go back to Norway? I asked. Yes, she had to—half her books were still there.

Back to Maysoon: After two sets she closed the evening with a pitch for a charity she has organized—

schooling for handicapped Palestinian kids in refugee camps—and a final line that got enormous applause: "Next year in Jerusalem!" Strange to hear the old hopeful/hopeless diasporic shibboleth on other than Jewish lips, and now freighted with a new urgency.

13 February: Cairo

In case you were wondering how the news from Egypt was affecting Ramallah: The Palestinian Authority, uncertain how to respond to these developments and fearing it might be the next Authority to be put in question, had forcibly broken up earlier rallies and bumped *Al-Jazeera*'s enthusiastic coverage off local TV. But yesterday was the 29th anniversary of the founding of the Palestinian People's Party, the renamed Communist

Party, allied to the PLO. (You can find its history on Wikipedia; it polled between 2% and 3% of the vote in the last election.) So there was a largish parade (about 500 people with a sound truck and banners) during lunch hour down into Al-Manara, Ramallah's central square with its famous stone lions (one, oddly, equipped with a stone wristwatch).

Note the marcher carrying an image of Nasser. There was a piece in *Al-Jazeera* yesterday on Nasser as a symbol of 1960s pan-Arabism, brought back in a new version, stressing human rights rather than freedom from colonial domination.

16 February: garbage

I was introduced to one of the university's vice-presidents the other day, a philosopher who enjoys—I was to learn—grilling newcomers in a jokey, provocative way. Learning that I was teaching one of my courses for the Urban Studies major, he asked what were my "qualifications."

"Twenty-seven years in Baltimore," I replied. "Those are not qualifications," he quipped, "those are facts."

True, but the fact remains that I look at cities through the lens of Baltimore. When I see a mural celebrating the struggle of the Palestinians under occupation, I think of the mosaic on Pennsylvania Avenue, in West Baltimore, honoring the first graduate of a drug rehab program. But the

resemblances of the West Bank to West Baltimore can be misleading in any number of ways and I'm nervous about invoking them, even though Palestinians have no hesitation in referring to the Occupation as a ghettoization. The issue arose again around the question of garbage, which is pervasive here. I had noticed how the upscale villas and condos in the East Jerusalem neighborhood of Shu'fat were often surrounded by stony lots laced with litter. My co-teacher, Omar Yousef, had explained then that although the Palestinian owners of those villas pay the same municipal taxes as other Jerusalemites, they don't receive the same services. That made sense, but what of Ramallah, where it is the Palestinian Authority who should be picking up the trash? I suppose one could argue that waste management is an expensive process, and the PA is often struggling to stay solvent. But the question is not so much why isn't trash picked up as why is it where it is in the first place: who put it there? Take, for example, the people who live in this villa in my neighborhood. Notice their tidy back yard, with its children's swing set. Then look at the garbage dumped over their wall into the lot next door. Only they would have had access to that spot in the wall. Do they just routinely chuck stuff there and then ignore it, once it lands a few feet below eye level?

I talked all this over with Omar and we decided to raise the question in class and see what our students had to say about it. One of them had written a nicely detailed description of her neighborhood along the Ramallah road, noting that her family's house was next to what she called a "garbage yard." No one seemed to think that was an unusual designation. So what do you make of this, we asked. The first explanation we were offered was cultural: Arabs, one student said (and others agreed) have a strong sense of the difference between what's inside the walls of a house and yard and what's outside. A carefully decorated and spotlessly clean interior might be surrounded by as it were invisible or at least unnoticed trash beyond the edge of the property.

As the discussion went on, other factors were cited, chief among them the Occupation, and the sense Palestinians have that public space is not "theirs," but belongs, however illegitimately, to the Israelis. The

Baltimore equivalent would presumably be the sense of disenfranchisement, of non-ownership, felt by residents of poor African-American neighborhoods. There was a time in the 90's when many mayors and police commissioners (chief among them Rudy Giuliani in New York and Commissioner James Bratton) were pinning their hopes for crime prevention on the Harvard sociologist James Q. Wilson's theory of "Broken Windows." The belief was that the crime rate would go down in neighborhoods that were kept tidy—broken windows in abandoned buildings repaired, litter picked up, etc. The theory had its dubious side and in fact is still being debated. But it prompted some comically inventive thinking in City Halls: in Baltimore, for example, which, at the time, was about 60% African-American, I remember wire trash cans appearing on corners with a perky message: *Slam Dunk One for Baltimore! Keep Our City Clean!* It was easy enough to imagine the brainstorming session downtown that had come up with this slogan: "Who litters?—Black teenagers.— What else do they like to do?—Shoot hoops.—So why don't we.......etc."

So, to return to Palestine: take a traditional but non-Western sense of public space; add the specific, contemporary (and disheartening) confusion about who "owns" this land—and here the analogy with West Baltimore becomes pertinent—then further add the expense of garbage collection. Could a combination of these factors explain the trash? And would suddenly renewed sense of enfranchisement account for the recent reports of the Egyptian protestors cleaning up Tahrir Square after Mubarak's fall? Omar tells me that on his earlier visits to Cairo he had had to wade through litter. Indeed, a similar set of factors may be behind the "garbage yards" I noticed walking through Mea She'arim, the ultra-Orthodox neighborhood in West Jerusalem. I'm told the residents there take their own distance from, have their own quarrels with, the municipal authorities, and have been known to act out their resentment by dumping and burning garbage.

Finally, a somewhat less bleak vignette. In Abu Dis, right across from the University's front gate, the pavement comes to a jagged edge and the land slopes down steeply. At the bottom of the slope are an unfinished building and a small villa, then the Wall. The slope itself is typical: part construction site, part garbage dump, a mix of rubbish and rubble. And for the fifteen minutes that I sat on the edge of the pavement the other

day, eating my lunch, two little girls—about 5 and 3—were working their way across the hillside, picking through the stones and the plastic bags, rescuing interesting items and carrying them about in a cardboard suitcase. Periodically, they would open the case, take things out—a red Coke can and some other

items—and line them up on the low wall, the border that marked where the dump left off and the villa's terrace began. Their resourcefulness had found resources in the waste.

The playthings in the playhouse of the children.
Weep for what little things could make them glad.

21 February: a beggar

After today's class, I hitch a ride with Omar toward his house on the Ramallah road in East Jerusalem, where I can catch a number 18 bus the rest of the way. It's beginning to rain heavily and strong winds are sweeping down the road, so he drops me at a sheltered bus stop. Well, partially sheltered; by the time the bus pulls up, I'm soaked. I've got a wet backpack over one shoulder and am carrying a bag of groceries and a kilo of goat meat (intended for a "lamb stew") in the other hand. I pay my fare, get some change and look back through the crowded bus. There are a couple of seats in the very back row, but a man closer by gestures for me to sit in the empty seat next to him. I get settled on his right as he extends his left hand in greeting: that would be a friendly gesture in France, "la main du coeur," but it's not the custom here. Puzzling, but then I realize that he has no right hand, no right arm. He goes on to explain, in fragments of English, that he lost it in the second Intifada. "Israelis," he says, "Israelis crazy." He pulls his leather jacket off his right shoulder, pulls his polo shirt collar off to the side and reveals the infolded stump of his upper arm. He points his left thumb and forefinger like a child pointing a make-believe revolver. He was shot in the arm? He nods his head: "Israelis crazy!" I nod in agreement. But it's clear now that he's making a pitch. (Here we go again, I think: as my family knows, I collect beggars as furniture collects dust.) He gestures towards his mouth then holds out his left hand, palm up. I drop the change I'd just received from the bus driver into it, a few shekels. He looks disappointed and continues the conversation. "Where are you from?" America, I tell him, New York, but not New York City, north, way north, 400 kilometers north: I draw a map with my forefinger on the back of the seat in front of us. He says something about Obama, adding something that sounds like "Hussein" and I nod, yes, Barack Hussein Obama. From Africa? he asks. No, from Hawaii: I locate "Hawaii" on the map, off to the west, near the steamed-up window. Is he approving of our president? That's the way such rudimentary conversations have gone in the past. But perhaps not; our president has just chosen to use his veto in the Security Council in the interests of Israel, not the Palestinians. Is my new friend aware of that? How can he not be, it's in all the papers and—as I will learn later in the evening from *The Guardian*'s website—a "Day of Rage" protesting the veto is planned in the West Bank for next Friday. My seatmate is back to the matter of money: he is talking of his children, three of them, holding up three of his remaining fingers. He moves them towards his mouth again, then into the thumb-and-bunched-fingers universal sign for "money." I tell him that when we get to Ramallah I will give him something more. He leans his head against the curtained window—the cold rain is still beating on the bus—and seems to doze off. By now we're approaching the Qalandia check-point, on the outskirts of Ramallah, a passage that shouldn't take long in this direction; it's the traffic headed towards Jerusalem that the Israelis are concerned about. But it takes an intolerably long time this evening. Partly it's the rain, partly it's the rush hour traffic, but mostly it's the labyrinthine structure of the checkpoint itself, a series of roundabouts that oblige incoming cars to twist back and around several times, getting in each other's way, before actually heading straight in the direction of Ramallah. It's dark, the windows are fogged, the bus is creeping ahead. My friend is asleep. And my irritation with the pressure of his need, real or feigned, is getting to me. Israelis crazy.

2 March: Ramallah's almond trees are in bloom

5 March: from Mount Scopus to Sheikh Jarrah

The sociologist Elijah Anderson, writing of how people deal with each other on the sidewalks of a mixed-income, mixed-race neighborhood in Philadelphia, notes how much mental energy has to go into keeping things feeling "normal" in places where people's suspicion and fear inform their interactions. I was thinking of this yesterday as the #18 bus, on its way to Jerusalem, slowed down for the routine inspection at the Qalandia checkpoint. Younger people and those with problematic documentation get off to make their way through the  cattle chute, the turnstiles and metal detectors on foot, past the blasé Israeli guards. The rest of us elders wait for a pair of armed inspectors—usually a college-age Israeli woman in uniform and a private security guy in jeans and dark glasses—to come down the aisle with their Uzis over their shoulders, frozen-faced, glancing at IDs and passports. It's infuriating, but the Palestinians, used to all this, don't seem infuriated, just mildly anxious. How many ergs, I wondered, are expended maintaining that cool?

I was on my way to the Hebrew University Library at Mount Scopus, which I had imagined would stay open—like kosher butchers in New York—at least until mid-afternoon on a Friday. But I was wrong: everything was closed down, so I wound up wandering around a series of connected, almost deserted buildings, looking for lunch. Like Abu Dis, but for different reasons, there's no Collegetown on Mount Scopus. It is focused inward and (except on the Sabbath) self-sufficient as a community: a handsome maze on a hilltop, each structure, each segment of each structure, bearing its plaque thanking its donor, the whole surrounded by well-tended gardens, just now vivid with blossoming almond trees. I found a coffee cart and got into conversation with its only other customer, a tall serious-looking man in his mid-thirties. He was a CPA, he told me, but studying for a degree in finance, and though he was only wearing a small black yarmulke he identified himself as ultra-Orthodox. I was puzzled: I'd thought he would be wearing more signs of his devotion, at least a fringed scapular if not the Full Hasidic Monty. He explained that no, there were different sects, and more and more ultra-Orthodox were entering the work force. He himself was not entirely comfortable with this, but "in his heart" he considered himself ultra-Orthodox. He had four children, but even his wife worked as a professor at an ultra-Orthodox school. He was surprised to find I was living in Ramallah and wondered what the town was like: was it still so poor? (He had last visited it years ago, during his military service.) I said no, it was actually pretty lively, with a lot of construction going on, and then—still sour from Qalandia and figuring "What can I lose?"—went on to tell him what I thought about The Occupation, the Wall, the routine humiliations at the checkpoints, etc., etc., all this in an amiable fashion. So an amiable conversation ensued. His English was labored, and he was anxious to convince me of his good intentions: yes, the checkpoints were humiliating, but then there was the question of security. The balance between respect for the Palestinians "as people" and the need to prevent violence had to be carefully maintained: when Israeli vigilance went down, he claimed, the suicide bombings went up. He regretted this, but seemed pleased with the clarity of the formula he had come up with (he was not a CPA for nothing). He recalled his uncomfortable feelings as a soldier on checkpoint duty. His two hands came out in appeal, then went back to his chest: he was clearly of two hearts about the matter, and was hoping I would understand. We parted politely: "Shabbat shalom."

It was early afternoon, and I still had a couple of hours before I was to meet friends at the weekly Friday afternoon demonstration in Sheikh Jarrah. I had time to walk down Mt. Scopus and further downhill through Wadi al-Joz—a bleak, sunny stretch of stone masons and automobile repair shops—then up again to the Old City. Crowds of Palestinians were moving in the opposite direction, carrying purchases they had made after midday prayers at the Al-Aqsa mosque.

My connection with the Sheikh Jarrah protests was accidental. A few summers ago, sitting at a café on the Cornell campus, I had shared a table with a young woman and her small child. She turned out to be the wife of an Israeli post-doc working on psychoanalysis and literature; she herself was a musicologist. This is a small country, in some circles a small world: I ran into her and her husband at a string quartet concert in Jerusalem shortly after I arrived and learned about the protests from them. In the summer of 2009, some Palestinian families were summarily—in a matter of minutes—evicted from their houses in a traditionally Arab district of East Jerusalem and immediately replaced by a group of right-wing settlers. Since then, that neighborhood has become the occasion for various kinds of confrontation—in the courts and on the street—involving lawyers and activists demanding justice for the original Palestinian homeowners and for others in the area threatened with eviction. (The activists' website—www.en.justjlm.org—can give you more detailed information. The group has also published a brochure relating in some detail the history of the legal claims and evictions, from which I've copied an Agence  France Press photo illustrating a particularly nasty, but not uncharacteristic, moment in relations between the neighborhood's remaining Palestinians and the settler youth who would have them leave.)

The Friday afternoon demonstrations have been going on for more than a year. There is a small public park, with an arbor and a low stone wall for seating, across from the entrance to the street where the settlers have now been settled. Several hundred people gather there around three. If the weather is fine, the atmosphere is festive. Teenage Palestinian vendors hawk freshly squeezed orange juice from carts. The mostly Israeli crowd, about evenly divided between young people and older types, elderly lefties in jeans and baseball caps, others with yarmulkes, greet each other, and, gradually, the rally starts: placards to display to passing cars, a bullhorn for chants, drumming, then a parade through the neighborhood. The two earlier times I'd attended, the police had formed a cordon blocking access to the settlers' homes, but this time the parade was allowed to head down the street and take its chanting right in front of one of the disputed houses. To get a better view of the crowd, I was standing on some steps leading into the back garden of an adjacent settler-controlled property. It was fenced off and its iron gate was locked; on the garden side of the fence blue plastic had been put up as a curtain, but the afternoon sun was low and bright behind the house and shadows of its new residents flashed on the wavering blue sheets. The chanting and drumming got louder, then abruptly the police, who'd been observing from the other side of the street, decided to move in to break things up, and, jogging in single file, they pushed their way through the crowd. A tussle ensued, more shouts, a cry of pain, arrests were being made, and then the police emerged with their handcuffed perps, followed by the drummer

 giving the squad car a *fortissimo* send-off, followed by people with cell phones and video cameras

documenting the scene, including a young Haredi settler. Then the rally broke up; people drifted back to the park, and I headed for a nearby bus stop. I was overtaken by a man I'd talked with earlier, there with his seven- or eight-year-old son. He worked for a human

rights NGO, he told me, one concerned with investigat-
ing allegations of torture. He had seen me photograph-
ing the arrest and asked if I would e-mail him a copy of
the image. As we talked he noticed that his son was
looking troubled, and asked him if he'd been frightened
by all the commotion on the steps. The boy nodded; he
had been. I stifled a grandfatherly/teacherly wish to tell
them both that that was good, that it was good to say
you were frightened when you were frightened, rather
than to pretend you weren't. Suppressing one's fear
takes too much energy.

15 March: the Tarifis, Itamar murders

Time to pay my rent. I walk around the corner
to the storefront office of Al-Tarifi Real Estate, the
owners of my building and of the other shops alongside
theirs—a sweetshop, a dry cleaner's, a pharmacy, a
bakery, a minimart and a now defunct café, soon to be
something else, I'm told. It's too bad about the café,
named, its owner told me, The Birth Café in honor of
the rebirth of Ramallah after the withdrawal of the IDF
some years ago. He was a slight man in his thirties with
a large, strikingly thin, salient nose that made him look
like a scaled-down version of Wilfred Hyde-White, the
great, urbane British character actor. The café owner
was urbane in his own right. He had a university degree,
had traveled, spoke several languages, but could find no
serious professional work in the West Bank. He'd take
the proceeds of selling his restaurant equipment and put
it into a clothing shop he owned elsewhere in Ramallah,
he told me. He was a skilled cook: I'd had some good
meals there in the days before he closed the place down,

sitting in this too dark, lounge-like setting, and talking with him—(I was usually his only customer). He liked novels, and wanted me to recommend some in English: I'd suggested Robert Stone's *Damascus Gate* and Don DeLillo's *The Names*, thinking he knew enough about the Middle East, and the world, to appreciate them. On politics, on "the Situation," he was a pessimist, though he was enthusiastic about what was happening in Egypt these last weeks.

We talked about the neighborhood and I told him I enjoyed dealing with the Tarifis, his landlords and mine, which surprised him. He saw them as too concerned with money—perhaps the judgment of a tenant on the verge of losing his lease. And it could be true, but still my visits to their office—to ask for a better reading lamp, to borrow a vacuum cleaner, to (mistakenly) report a leak in the propane tank—have been a pleasure. My actual landlord, Khaled, the man who signed my lease, is the oldest of ten children of a man whose family, in 1948, was driven out of a village named Tarif. (No way to find it on a contemporary map—it was demolished). Since then members of the family—Khaled, his parents, and at least one of his siblings—have spent time on the Near North Side of Chicago, and it shows: except for his father's puffing on a waterpipe instead of a cigar, as he holds court in the front room of the narrow suite of offices, chatting but keeping an eye on the street, we could be in the opening chapters of *Augie March*: the Old Man, his sons, the young building manager learning the ropes, a couple of other gofers, some drop-ins and hangers-on, a family operation, a very recognizable big city American scene. But of course I'm putting the cart before the horse: family operations of this sort were imported to America

from the Middle East, from Italy, from Poland, from
China, long before I ran into them in the Manhattan of
my childhood, or in Bellow's Chicago.

Today, when I arrive with my wad of 200-shekel
notes, the Old Man isn't around, and I find Khaled alone
with his brother and Nazeeh, the super, in the back
office, which is better furnished, with some Islamic art
on the walls and the apparatus of business—file cabinets
and a large-screened computer. We talk about Libya, and
then I get around to what I really wanted to know: what
they'd heard about the bloody knife-killing of a Jewish
family, a mother, a father, and three sleeping children, at
Itamar, a settlement near Nablus, about 20 miles north
of Ramallah. For the last couple of days it has been *the*
major news in Israel, even in competition with what's
happening in Libya or with the scenes of unimaginable
terror and misery broadcast from Japan. The Israeli
government's response was to immediately approve the
building of 500 more housing units on the West Bank—
(as if they might *not* have done so if these murders hadn't
taken place?)—and, among other statements of anger
and concern, to lodge an official protest with CNN for
using the word "intruders" instead of "terrorists" when
describing the killers. This was drearily predictable, but
so, I discovered, was the Tarifis' response: what about all
the children the Israelis had killed in Gaza, what about all
the settler violence? In fact, Khaled's brother said, one of
the killers was a man whose son had been shot by settlers
two or three years ago. I wondered how he could know
that: the killers haven't yet been caught or even identified; the IDF is still rounding up suspects. This must be
something people are telling one another. But whether
it's true or not, it too is predictable. Had I challenged
this report, I would have been asked what difference it

made whether it was actually this man's son or some other man's son: children, sons are being killed. Victims are interchangeable units in the prevailing local calculus: it's not *this* eye for *that* eye, but any eye for any eye, any tooth, any arm, any child. That's as far as I could press the question with the Tarifis. If I want to learn more of what to expect in the way of a Palestinian response to the Israeli response to the murders—and, living as I do in Ramallah, this is not a matter of idle curiosity—I shall have to ask people who can more fully take in the local news. There's a limit to what I can get from *Ha'aretz*'s and *Al-Jazeera*'s English editions.

Actually, a sentence in *Ha'aretz*'s initial report, about how the Itamar settlement was famous for its bad relations with its Arab neighbors, set me to reading more about the Fogels, the family who were killed, about Itamar, and about the so-called Religious Zionists who founded the colony in 1984. They are associated with the Machon Meir yeshiva in Jerusalem, whose chief rabbi was a student of the better-known Rabbi Zvi Yehuda Kook (1891-1982) who led the Mercaz HaRav yeshiva, also in Jerusalem, founded by his still more famous father, Rabbi Abraham Isaac Kook (1865-1935). Father and son, these rabbis preached the Redemption of the Land, carrying forward a line of rabbinical thought that predates Herzl's founding of the Zionist movement in the late nineteenth-century, (a line of thought that George Eliot read her way into when composing *Daniel Deronda*). The younger Kook is considered the spiritual founder of the post-1967 settler movement. There had been many earlier settlements in the West Bank, even long before 1948, but they proliferated after Israel captured control of that territory in 1967.

Attempts are often made to discriminate between violent and non-violent settlers. In a video interview circulating just now, the father murdered in his bed, Udi Fogel, in fact comes across as a sweet-natured man, once a tank commander, now a farmer and teacher. And yesterday some members of the Itamar community insisted on their non-violent ethos: they were grieving but they were not angry, they said; and they never demonstrated, they never attacked the Arab villagers; it was "those crazies on the hilltop," other (more radical) Zionist youth, encamped above them, who did things like that; Itamar families simply wanted to be left alone in this their homeland to study Torah, grow organic vegetables, and raise their kids, plus some sheep and goats. Last night, however, the IDF had to intervene to keep some masked Itamar settlers from taking revenge on the nearby Palestinian village of Awarta, downhill from the settlement. And a history of Itamar notes that one of its founders was the son of a member of the "Jewish Underground" movement who, in 1984, was convicted of plotting to blow up the Dome of the Rock, so as to clear the way for the building of the Third Temple on what some believe to be Solomon's Temple's original site. (More of this below). Past a certain point, distinguishing between "nice" and "nasty" settlers, legitimate or illegitimate acts of resistance on the Palestinians' part, makes little sense: the violence is structural, inherent in the project of Redeeming the Land.

Recently, I came across a remarkably apropos bit of autobiographical writing when preparing a reader for the course Omar Yousef and I are teaching on Jerusalem. It speaks to the compelling force, for some Israelis, of the Redemptive project. In a book called

Jewish Fundamentalism and the Temple Mount: Who Will Build the Third Temple? the Israeli historian Motti Imbari devotes a chapter to a Messianic organization founded in 1984 called The Temple Institute and to its leader, Rabbi Israel Ariel. Imbari is interested in producing a psychohistorical account of the vicissitudes of Messianic thinking in present-day Israel. He believes that Ariel was impelled to found The Temple Institute by a particular experience during the 1967 war, when he was a paratrooper in a unit fighting its way towards the Western Wall of the Temple Mount. As he got closer to the Wall he heard from some soldiers in front of him that they had run into "two old men" up ahead. And here Imbari quotes Ariel's memoir:

> I thought to myself: The Messiah and the Prophet Elijah must have arrived. Who else could appear here during the battle for the Temple Mount after two thousand years? That was what seemed natural at the time. [....] Naturally, the two old men who should appear at this time are the Messiah and the Prophet Elijah. So I went off to meet the Messiah and the Prophet Elijah. I asked myself where I would find them. Surely on the Temple Mount— they must have come to build the Temple. But I saw everyone running toward the Western Wall.
>
> For some reason people were more moved by the wall than by the Temple Mount. Awareness of the Western Wall is much greater among the people than awareness of the Temple [....]
>
> I arrived at the Western Wall, and below me I saw two old men—none other than my two rabbis and teachers from the yeshiva, Rabbi Zvi Yehuda Kook (may the memory of the righteous be blessed!) and the "Reclusive Rabbi" (may the memory of the righteous be blessed!). We embraced and stood with

tears running down our cheeks, in complete silence, sensing that Messiah was still on the way—it would just take another hour or two.

In 1967 Rabbi Zvi Yehuda Kook was 76 years old, a venerable (and much venerated) "old man," but not, as it turned out, the Messiah. According to Imbari, the psychohistorian, it would take decades for Ariel to work through his experience that day—the sacred thrill of expectation, the ensuing disappointment—and reinterpret it as a vocation, an understanding of his mission. He had wrongly imagined that the Messiah had come to rebuild the Temple; he now understood that it was only when the Temple was rebuilt that the Messiah would come. He was called to hasten that moment, whence the Temple Institute. Imbari also notes that in 1984 Ariel founded a journal that was devoted to justifying the actions of those convicted of the attempt on the Al-Aqsa Mosque and to "encouraging the expectation of the construction of the Temple."

Someone takes a knife and kills a family in what seems like an act of archaic vengeance; someone else longs to blow up one holy site to replace it with one holier still—you can become hypnotized by such stories of tribal warfare into forgetting that other vocabularies of motivation may also apply and perhaps be even more pertinent. Suppose that the killings at Itamar are part of a quite coolheaded strategy on, say, Hamas's part to embarrass the Palestinian Authority at this particular juncture in their (currently non-violent) dealings with the Israelis; or consider that most Israeli political figures, from 1948 on, have not been theologically committed to the Redemptive project but have nevertheless quite cynically manipulated its capacity to excite popular ardor, and that the "real cause" of the Arab/Israeli conflict may be better located in the question of who shall control the aquifers in the Jordan Valley.

22 March: the desert, a sick joke?

Omar drives me out from Abu Dis to have a look at the desert on the Jericho road. Parts of the landscape, he explains, have been naturally dessicated for years, other parched areas can be attributed to Israel's control of the waters of the Jordan aquifer, or to the destruction of olive groves, sometimes by settlers in surreptitious raids, at other times by the IDF, who have cleared groves adjacent to major highways because, they report, Palestinian kids stone passing cars, then  hide in among the trees. Further along we reach The Inn of the Good Samaritan and turn in to its parking lot. No succor here in

this season: the restaurant is closed, and we're waved away by a security man. Across from the parking lot, however, we spot a strange construction, a whimsical serpentine path leading up to a yet-to-be-completed pedestrian bridge over the highway. Can this be somebody's idea of a (sick) joke about the Wall? Omar, less hysterical than I, thinks not. But then, what else might it be? A surprisingly located tribute to Sherlock Holmes and "The Adventure of the Speckled Band"?

24 March: "Du rififi chez les hommes"

That's the title of the great 1950's Jules Dassin film about a jewel-heist gone bad and the vendetta that ensued. Loosely translated, it might be *The Boys Are At It Again*. In what we thought was a thorough risk-assessment last fall, my wife and I had come up with a list of various ways I might get in trouble over here—by mouthing off to some guard at a checkpoint (the Israeli option), by being mistaken for a settler (the Palestinian option), even (call it the Baltimore option) by getting merely mugged. In our innocence, or our wishfulness, we hadn't factored in the kind of bombing that just took place near the West Jerusalem bus station. It's too early to tell how that is going to change how people live their lives over here: I'm sure I'll have more to say about that as time goes on. For the moment, here's something else that had never occurred to us—finding oneself in the midst of feuding clans.

Last Thursday (part of the weekend for the AQB program, so neither our faculty nor our students were on campus) a gang from the neighboring village of Sawahira came over to Abu Dis, torched a café and a bookstore across from the main gate of the Al-Quds campus, then had come through the gate, shooting

 randomly. Several students were hospitalized with gunshot wounds. What was this all about? I've found it hard to get a straight answer.

When I came to work last Saturday, I asked the Palestinian security guard at the main gate what had gone on. "Ach," he said, "Arabs." I'd heard that knowing tone once before, on the Ramallah bus one night, when a hopped-up twenty-something got into a fight with the driver. "Get outta my bus," the driver shouted, getting up and heading down the aisle to confront the passenger. My burly Palestinian seatmate stood and pushed them apart, then, sitting back down, turned to me and said, in English, "Arabs," with a rueful smile that suggested that, while he deplored this macho violence, he recognized, even partially identified with, its "characteristic" bravado: our well-known hot blood.

So what had "in fact," happened? It's been a week now, and I can't say I've gotten a clear answer, though lots of people are talking about the violence. There have, it seems, been incidents like this before, including one sometime last fall. Abu Dis and Sawahira are rival villages with, it's said, rival "clans" or "tribes" or "families" (in both the kinship sense and the Mafia sense of "family"). This time the fight was about the building that housed the bookstore and the café. The people from Sawahira claimed that the building—still unfinished: it can be seen on the left of the photo, in an earlier post, of the two little girls gathering toys in the rubble— impinged (to the extent of a couple of meters) on land belonging to Sawahira. They had sent an emissary over to make this claim and he had been badly beaten (there's a grim video showing this beating on the plaza in front of the University). The torching of the café was their revenge. But why then shoot up the campus? I've heard various explanations more or less lurid: that "some people" have it in for the University, that the shooters may even have been Israelis. (To the student who came up with this account, I asked: But can't you tell Israelis from Palestinians? His answer: But they were masked!) This version seemed less likely than one claiming that the head of the Sawahira family was a notorious drug-dealer, and this may have been about more serious "territory" than the alleged couple of meters. And that's where things stand. Classes are back in session. The Student Council had considered calling a strike demanding better campus security but called it off, presumably because they'd received assurances from the administration that something would be done. The University may even have issued some calming pronouncement, like the letters one receives from American university presidents in similar situations, expressing sympathy for the victims of violence ("and their families") and calling for everyone to rededicate themselves to their studies, to their teaching and research and community service, those primary missions of the university "family." Ach, families!

25 March: The Arab Spring—an emblem

     Ben Ali, Mubarak, Qaddafi, Saleh...... Assad? Mohammed II? Abbas? Netanyahu??

     as when the sun new risen
Looks through the horizontal misty air
Shorn of his beams, or from behind the moon
In dim eclipse disastrous twilight sheds
On half the nations, and with fear of change
Perplexes monarchs.

                      [*Paradise Lost*, 1.594 ff.]

27 March: more on the feud

This afternoon, I took a cab down to an Apple store just off the Ramallah-Jerusalem road, then, since the weather had warmed up overnight, decided to make the long walk home, taking some pictures along the way. I hoped to get a good image of the combination of residual olive groves, half-completed, abandoned shells of housing, and upscale postmodern office towers that's been characteristic of Ramallah in the last few years and gives the town its cluttered, faux-solid, provisional look.

Today was a Saturday, ordinarily a teaching day, but I'd learned early in the morning that the campus would be closed, at least for a day, possibly more: the man from Sawahira who was so badly beaten just outside the University gate last week had died in hospital, and it was feared that his relatives might return to Abu Dis to take their revenge. I was standing in front of a blue glass-and-cement tower, wondering whether it was housed government or corporate offices (the building across from it had elaborate signs announcing that Novartis and other pharmaceutical firms had their suites there), when I got into conversation with a thirty-ish man out walking with his small children. He answered my questions about the building and invited me to walk along with them. He was carrying his two-year-old and urging on a sulky four-year-old who was lagging behind.

This young father's name was Salim. He was a manager, he said, at a nearby Palestinian firm, but this was his day off. His wife was at work, though, so he was taking care of the boys and was clearly glad of some adult company. We talked partly in English, partly in French—he was from a village near Hebron, had gone to university there, but later had spent some time in Moulins, in the Auvergne, as a worker in an NGO. It soon became clear that he was inviting me home; we climbed away from the main road, then down again into a hollow where he stopped for supplies at a small grocery, then up the seven cold flights of his building's stairway to a four-room apartment with a balcony overlooking the shallow valley that runs parallel to the main drag just over the hump to its west. We'd been talking about Al-Quds—we had just walked past the University's Ramallah campus housing its School of Media Studies—and as we were getting settled in his apartment I mentioned the reason the school had called off classes today. He was startled. He'd known about the beating, but hadn't heard this latest bit: "You mean the guy died??" he said, and immediately went to the phone. Hanging up, he said he had called his father-in-law in Sawahira, who had confirmed the death. My new friend's wife, it turned out, was from this notorious village, and in fact knew the dead man, Saher Mashahara, by name. One thing his father-in-law had told him was that the funeral had not yet taken place: first the vendetta, then the burial, was the way things were customarily done in Sawahira.

Salim invited me to stay for "lunch," but I hesitated. It was by now mid-afternoon, I was tired, the apartment was cold, the kids were charming but rambunctious, needing constant attention—the four-year-old, Mamdouh, had learned how to open the breaker-switch panel high on the kitchen wall and was, at one point, about to insert his father's house-key into one of the slots. I yelled a warning and he got a slap. I wanted to go home; but I also wanted to meet this wife, this daughter of Sawahira; plus, I liked the looks of the chicken dish Salim was preparing as we talked. So I stayed. The chicken cooked. The younger boy, Ra'eed, conked out in his crib. Salim showed me slides of their trip, last September, to France—shots of the Louvre (the Mona Lisa, David's "The Oath of the Horatii"), of a boat ride on the Seine, of his old friends in Moulins whom he'd taken his family to meet. I asked if the Occupation made such travel difficult, getting to Tel Aviv, for example, to take the plane. There was no problem, no problem: they fly from Amman. Finally Rana, the wife and mother, returned—head-scarf, nicely tailored long outer robe, alert eyes, wide smile, but quick to discipline her boys, and not all that gently. After greeting me she spoke briefly with Salim then disappeared into the bedroom. I could hear her voice and wondered if she was praying. But no, she was talking to her best friend in Sawahira, getting the news. So now I'm in a position to tell, with some authority, why Al-Quds University's Abu Dis campus was closed today:

Saher Mashahara's wife was from an Abu Dis family, the Jaffals, and her father had given her—as a wedding gift?—some land near the University, presumably the land where the half-finished (and now torched) building housing the café and bookstore stands. But the land, it seemed, was not really the Jaffals to bestow; part of it belonged to another Abu Dis family, the Muhlems. So they, the Muhlems, had argued with Saher about this and members of Saher's family had come to Abu Dis and beaten up a Muhlem. The video showed what ensued: the Muhlems dragging Saher out of his car next time he came to Abu Dis and beating him to the ground. He was in his late twenties and leaves a wife and three kids. Neither Salim nor Rana could explain why the Sawahira gang then came through the University gates and started shooting; they imagined that some Al-Quds students from Abu Dis may have been targeted. Salim said (confirming what I'd heard, indirectly, from a friend in Cambridge, who'd heard it from a friend in Tel Aviv, who'd heard it from the journalist Amira Hass) that the Sawahiras were, originally, Bedouins, and went on to tell a story of a strong-armed patriarch laying claim to some Abu Dis land, a story that dated back to the pre-1918 days of Ottoman rule. After "lunch"—it was now around five—Rana excused herself to go off and see a woman friend. I remarked to Salim that he had a gracious and hospitable wife. Sawahira people are famous for their hospitality, he said. I must have looked surprised, for "Oh yes," he went on, there's an old Bedouin saying—and he chanted the rhymed lines in Arabic, roughly translated as "Give all you've got to your guests and beat your enemies with all your might!" I think I'd run into that sentiment somewhere in the pages of Doughty's *Travels in Arabia Deserta*. Or in an episode of *The Sopranos*. Or from a colleague embroiled in one of the bloodless vendettas of academic life. No word, as I write, of whether school's back in session tomorrow.

29 March: seatbelt protocol

The Palestinian Authority requires that all riders in the service minibuses use their seat belts, and there are heavy fines for being caught without your belt buckled (and a yet heavier fine for your driver). But it's assumed that only the IDF takes the ruling seriously, and does so less out of concern for riders' safety than because it provides yet another way of hassling

Palestinian traffic. So the routine practice is this: a few miles south of Ramallah, just as we're slowing down for a minor checkpoint near a hilltop settlement, the driver reminds us to buckle our belts. We do, and keep them on for the bulk of the trip, much of it, it should be conceded, along some steep and curving stretches of highway, usually taken at pretty high speed by our drivers, who have an incentive to make each trip quickly, turn around and make another. Each of the seven passengers will pay 12 shekels (about three dollars) for the ride from Ramallah to Abu Dis, so the more 84-shekel runs a driver can get in, the better. The drivers are generally skillful and clever and they don't take chances on the curves. Only once have I been scared enough to get one of the drivers to let me off at a crossroads half-way home. The other passengers were amused but sympathetic: *majnoon*, they agreed: he's crazy. I waited a while and caught another ride back to town.

The highway ends at the traffic circle leading (for Israelis) into the major settlement of Ma'ale Adumim or (for Palestinians) into Azaria. We slow down, negotiate the circle and head into Azaria's main drag, the old road from Jerusalem to Jericho, now blocked off by The Wall at the other end of Azaria, so no longer serving as a thoroughfare but rather as a busy Palestinian shopping strip. We pass a sign telling Israelis they may not enter this area, under Palestinian Authority administrative control—and then, unostentatiously, with no great sighs of relief but nevertheless purposefully, we all—led by the driver himself—unbuckle our safety belts and push them aside. A couple of blocks in we turn left at the newly built mosque and plunge into the ravine that separates

Azaria from Abu Dis. The road narrows, the curves are tighter, the drop beyond the shoulder more precipitous. No one moves to rebuckle his seat belt.

Like the deadly Norwegian sardines in the old joke—"You mean they *ate* those sardines??? Those sardines weren't for *eating*! They were for *buying and selling*!!"—safety belts on the West Bank aren't for safety, they're for making minor but endlessly satisfying micropolitical gestures.

1 April: vestiges of the Mandate: cloth

On the way home, our minibus stops to pick up a black-clad middle-aged woman waiting at the junction of Route 1 (leading east to Jericho and Jordan) and Route 437, which swings northwest to Ramallah. She climbs in and sits beside me, telling the driver to be on the lookout for her husband, who will be joining us down the line. And so he does after a while, and his wife gets out briefly so that he can squeeze in and occupy the seat between us. Then for the rest of the trip I find myself sitting shoulder to shoulder with a glen plaid jacket. This man was wearing Western trousers, but

it's common in East Jerusalem and the West Bank to see older men in red-and-white checked Palestinian *kaffiyehs* and the long gowns called *abayahs*, the equivalent of their wives embroidered *thobs*, wearing wool jackets—Harris tweeds, worsteds, herringbones—tailored in the old three-button, "natural-shoulder" style that is getting harder and harder to find even in Anglophile temples like J. Press or Brooks Bros. I'm guessing that the adoption of sports jackets by Westernizing Arabs must be a legacy of the British Mandate here (1918-1947).

3 April: Student Council

For whatever reasons—the demoralizing effect of the Occupation, the divisions within and among their leading political parties—Palestinians have not taken the events in Tunisia, Egypt, Yemen, Bahrain, Libya, Syria and Jordan as a signal for a mass movement of their own. I've noted an early attempt to hold a demonstration in Al-Manara, Ramallah's main square that was quickly—and violently—broken up by the

Palestinian Authority police. More recently, as I mentioned, the PA relented and allowed a parade and demo, ostensibly celebrating the anniversary of the Communist Party but really an outlet for genuinely strong popular feelings of support for what was happening in Cairo's Tahrir Square. Later, in mid-March, there would be another gathering with a catch-all agenda, including a denunciation of Obama for using his veto in the Security Council against the Palestinians.

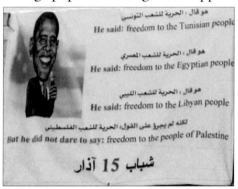

هو قال : الحرية للشعب التونسي
He said: freedom to the Tunisian people

هو قال : الحرية للشعب المصري
He said: freedom to the Egyptian people

هو قال : الحرية للشعب الليبي
He said: freedom to the Libyan people

لكنه لم يجرؤ على القول : الحرية للشعب الفلسطيني
But he did not dare to say: freedom to the people of Palestine

شباب 15 آذار

A few weeks ago, some young people began a hunger strike, denouncing the internecine struggles among Palestinian factions and calling for talks between Fatah and Hamas, the principal antagonists. They camped out in a makeshift tent alongside the Square, and hoisted a banner saying "Yes to Palestinian Unity." They were attacked twice, first by "thugs" who ripped down the lower half of the banner, leaving simply a big Arabic "Yes" (which was fine with the protestors), then, a few days later, by a group of students from Bir Zeit University, a few kilometers north of Ramallah. When I asked what that was all about, I was told that these were Fatah students, that their party had just won a Student Council election, and that this was their way of celebrating. Huh? A *Student Council* election?

I know there are undergraduates in America who dream of serious political power at an early age—the Bill Clintons, the Karl Roves—and who join the Young Republicans or the Young Democrats and run for Student Council, but the councils themselves are not organized around political parties. In Palestine they are, and serving on them is a step towards becoming a cadre in Hamas or Fatah or one of the smaller parties. But there is a further difference: the Palestinians have not voted in a national election since 2006, when Hamas won the majority of seats in the Legislative Council and was promptly "delegitimized" by Israel and the Quartet on the Middle East. Sanctions were imposed on the Palestinians: the deadly Gaza blockade would emerge from that reaction. So, for the last five years, the best indicators of Palestinian popular sentiment have been the results of Student Council elections on university campuses. Al-Quds is in the midst of its election right now. There are banners on all the buildings and hundreds of flags—stuck in the lawns, hung from trees, waved by bands of marching and hollering students.  Elegantly calligraphed posters proclaim the parties' slogans, but, according to Omar, they are vapid—the Palestinian equivalent of motherhood and apple pie. When the results are posted, I may be able to get some students to tell me what to make of it all.

16 April: more on the Itamar murders

The news this weekend was that the IDF has announced that they have arrested the killers of the Fogel family of Itamar. The suspects are two teenagers from the nearby village of Awarta who, according to reports, have confessed ("without showing any remorse") and even reenacted the crime in a visit back to the settlement. It appears there is DNA evidence, so the accusations have been accepted as valid, even by some Awarta villagers, although the boys' families are saying that the confessions were beaten out of them.

At the funeral for the family, back in March, Udi Fogel's brother, Motti, had said, addressing the body in the coffin, "You are gone. You are gone and no slogan can bring you back. Above all, this funeral must be a private event. Udi, you are not a symbol or a national event. Your life had a purpose of its own and your horrid death must not render that life into a vehicle." This was his hope, but it can hardly have been his expectation; he had just listened to the Chief Rabbi of Israel urging the 20,000 people in attendance to "Remember what Amalek did to you on the way as you came out of Egypt." (The reference is to *Deuteronomy* 25:17.) He went on: "Amalek is here!" and declared that "Itamar needs to become a major city in Israel." But I doubt that even Motti Fogel, so clearly wary of the appropriation of his grief for religious and political ends, could have imagined that his surviving nieces and nephew—a twelve year-old girl and her younger siblings—would, this past weekend, be given a "special briefing" on the success of the investigation by none other than the Chief of Staff of the IDF, who then had himself photographed presenting them with a commemorative volume—

a Passover Haggadah!
("Season's greetings,
kids!").

The photo
appeared in an early
on-line edition of
Ha'aretz. I couldn't
believe my eyes, and,

*I was unable to receive
permission from the IDF
to reprint this photo*

indeed, when I went back on-line a few hours later, to
try to download it, it had disappeared, replaced by a
montage of the two accused murderers and their five
victims. Nor did any mention of the Chief of Staff and
his Haggadah appear in the print version of *Ha'aretz*
this morning. Someone must have pointed out to the
IDF public relations people that this was perhaps "inap-
propriate," perhaps even a little "grotesque"?

22 April: another meal at Salim's

Salim, the young man whose wife's father lived
in Sawahira, near the house of the man who was beaten
to death in Abu Dis not long
ago, invited me for dinner
yesterday. Arriving in his
neighborhood too early to
knock on his door, I walked
around a bit among the
mixture of empty lots, villas,
apartment blocks and half-
finished buildings. It was a
cloudy and raw late afternoon,
but at one corner some kids
were kicking a ball around

until a friend rode up, bareback, on a handsome horse. Nearby, despite the weather, an ice cream truck was piping out ice cream truck music, "Happy Birthday to You" and "Jingle Bells." (The latter, it would seem, is a global favorite in any season: I'd listened to the same soundtrack playing on a broiling July day, in an air-conditioned bus taking tourists to the imperial tombs outside Beijing.) Down the street a mysterious gate spoke of Teletubbies: was this where they really lived or just where their Ramallan fans hung out?

Salim was late arriving home—he'd stopped to meet some friends at a downtown mosque—so I sat a while with Rana, exchanging fragments of English and Arabic, until he showed up. When he arrived we gathered around the dining room table while he chopped tomatoes and peppers for an Arabic salad to accompany the chicken-with-saffron-rice dish Rana had prepared earlier as the main course. A "Jewish" dish, he explained, called "Uzi"; he thought I'd be familiar with it. "You mean like the machine gun?" I asked. "Yes, it's a man's name." Salim is intent on demonstrating that he has nothing against Jews. He went on to say that there are Jewish settlers near the village he comes from, outside Hebron, who'd lived there for years on good terms with his family, and who deplore the actions of the more recent settlers. As he described them, I realized he was talking about ultra-Orthodox anti-Zionists, either Satmar Hasids or Neturei Karta, groups who believe that the establishment of a Jewish state prior to the arrival of the Messiah is a heresy. The more outspoken of the two, the Neterei Karta ("Guardians of the City") have achieved

some notoriety by endorsing Palestinian resistance. One of their rabbis had recently scandalized "World Jewry" when he appeared in Teheran with Ahmadinejad at a conference of Holocaust deniers. (In fact, according to Wikipedia, he went there to chide the conferees: the Holocaust was quite real, he is quoted as saying: his mother had died in Auschwitz. Does the concept of "strange bedfellows" have room for such arguments between the sheets?)

I asked Salim what he thought of the recently announced arrests of the two suspects in the Itamar murders. He said that he—and most of the people he'd talked with—believed it was a set-up, that they'd been tortured into confessing. He recalled that, at first, suspicion had fallen on some Thai workers in the settlement, and wondered why that possibility hadn't been pursued. "But what about the DNA evidence?" I was about to say, when I suddenly realized that, in spite of what I'd written in my last entry it wasn't completely clear to me that there *was* DNA evidence connecting the two suspects to the murders: all I've seen in *Ha'aretz* and elsewhere was that the IDF had collected DNA samples and fingerprints in Awarta. Have I missed an announcement that the evidence collected was probative? Could be. But my willingness to assume that it was probative, that, as they say in crime movies, the case was good as closed, was symmetrical to Salim's suspicion, shared by many Palestinians, that the two young men were being railroaded, despite the fact that they had, we are told, confessed.

[Postscript 29 January 2012: Whatever doubts Salim—or I—may have entertained about the guilt of the Awarta murderers of the Fogel family must be dispelled by the news, reported in today's Ha'aretz, that the mother and aunt of one of the teenagers appeared on a Palestinian TV show recently, praising the boy (now serving multiple life sentences in an Israeli prison) as "a hero and a legend."]

Salim is a worldly man who speaks Arabic, Hebrew, English and French, and who has no trouble distinguishing "Jews" or even "Israelis" from "Zionists." Yet he is convinced that there can be no justice for Palestinians in Israeli courts, just as he is convinced that there is no solution to "The Situation." It will just go on. What about all the recent events in the Middle East, I ask, won't that have some effect? Salim answered that what's happening in Libya is simply a Western attempt to carve up Arab territory, a replay of the Anglo-French dismantling of the Ottoman empire after the First World War. The fighting in Libya is being deliberately allowed to continue, he insisted, so that both sides will be exhausted, and the West can move in. "I believe in conspiracy theories," he said, with half a smile.

Before I left, I asked if there was any news from Sawahira. Yes, he said: the sixteen men who had beaten that fellow to death were in jail. Blood money—$150,000—had been paid to his widow, and a one-year truce between Sawahira and Abu Dis had been declared. And after that? I asked. After that, there will be revenge, he said, but the Sawahirans don't want to just kill some randomly chosen person from Abu Dis: they will wait for the 16 murderers to be released from jail. That's how it will be.

At first it had struck me as a remarkable bit of luck to have run into Salim in front of his postmodern office building on a street in Ramallah miles from Sawahira and Abu Dis, that particular day. It comes to seem a shade less improbable when you consider the current social evolution of the West Bank, where village life is becoming increasingly unsustainable and sons and daughters of village families, educated and uneducated, are drawn to the major cities—Ramallah, Nablus and Hebron. And this for the usual reasons that have been emptying out villages around the globe, but helped along in Palestine by the strictures of the Occupation, which make agricultural endeavors more and more difficult in a countryside laced with settlements and prohibitions.

27 April: a walk in the hills

I had earlier mentioned the Bir Zeit philosopher who had written a dissertation in Oslo on the Jerusalem poetry of Darwish and Amichai. We've stayed in touch—she will be speaking to our class in a couple of weeks—and yesterday she invited me and another friend out to her parents' house, in the hills north of Ramallah, for a walk and a meal. The hills are greener here than those I pass through on the way to Abu Dis and the village has been an olive-growing community, its trees climbing the steep terraced slopes surrounding the town. The minibus driver from Ramallah knew the family—he belonged to the same clan, knew my friend by her nickname—and promised to drop us off at her house for 70 shekels (about twenty dollars); then he rapidly negotiated the curves and drops of the roads leading north of Bir Zeit, snaking among settlements, a couple of unmanned checkpoints, a rural yeshiva and the usual mix of completed and semi-completed, isolated Palestinian concrete villas.

We set out on our walk almost immediately: our philosopher friend was going to take us up a hill where she'd walked many times with her late father, a man who had spent his life farming. The daughter, whom I'll call

Rima, is a witty, energetic, outgoing woman in her late thirties who, as far as I can tell, has never used the word "apparently" in any of the six or seven languages she speaks. She knows what she knows and she knows a great deal: on a country walk, the names and properties and edibility quotient of herbs and flowers, the varieties of olive trees, as well as the local history and lore.

We climbed slowly uphill, heading for the remains of an abandoned village on the summit which had been destroyed, Rima told us, in Ottoman times, for non-payment of taxes. Some herdsmen were sitting around taking in the view while their flocks grazed among the stones. On an eastern hilltop at some distance, one could make out Ari'el, one of the larger religious settlements. Closer by, Rima could point out yet others; her village is surrounded by Israeli posts. And the hilltop where we stood had, for the last few years, been marked out by settlers for further construction. She pointed out the coded red markings on the scattered Ottoman-era stones. The usual procedure was for groups of settlers to come out to a site for a "picnic"—we could see a circle of stones where a campfire had been lit. Then, once the spot is so designated, they would return fairly frequently, to maintain their "claim," before actually building anything there. Rima told us that it was only because we were taking our walk during the Passover holiday that we could be sure of not running into any settlers. Palestinian hikers, as well as the shepherds, stayed away from this hilltop  when there was any chance of encountering settlers. A real loss: the view across the valley is spectacular.

We made our way downhill and back to the family's villa, which they've only been in for the last couple of years. Rima had grown up in an older house, closer to the center of the village. This one was architect-designed under the supervision of Rima's sister; it's an elegant (and no doubt expensive) three-storey building with a large kitchen and open, airy living areas. Rima's mother—wearing a head scarf and the subdued colors favored by older, widowed Arab women—had prepared a chicken dinner for us, but would not join us at table. Afterwards other family members arrived, Rima's sister, her son and baby daughter, another cousin. An

 American soap opera was playing silently on the flat-screen television, subtitles in Arabic flashing beneath the open, too-vivid actors' faces. We sat around talking. I complimented Rima's sister on the design of the house and asked if she was herself an architect. No, it turned out that she was a businesswoman. She and her husband had owned a small factory in Gaza, which, after the blockade, they had moved north, to a site near Bir Zeit. They manufactured electrical equipment, specifically the recessed housings for ceiling lights. They bought most of their materials and machinery from China—in fact, she and her husband were on their way to the trade fair in Guangzhou in a couple of days. Did she speak Cantonese? I asked (a reasonable question in this household, given how many languages Rima has mastered); no, she said, but one can hire Arabic-Chinese interpreters over there. These sisters are three steps away from a village existence; their mother still lives that life, no longer farming but tending an elaborate herb garden in her backyard, while her daughters globalize.

It was time to think of heading back to Ramallah, although Rima's mother had hoped we would stay the night. We asked about finding a taxi back and talk turned to the driver who had brought us out. "How much did you say he charged you?" Rima asked. "Seventy shekels," we said. Great disapproval, and questions about who he was, exactly: was he a short guy in his thirties, rather slender? The family was sure they knew him—another clansman, so he shouldn't have asked that much to go to a cousin's house. "We're going to burn him!" Rima comically threatened. We were back in the tribal idiom, this time within quotation marks. As it turned out, Rima's sister drove us all back as far as Bir Zeit, pointing out her factory on the way. We wished her a successful trip to Guangzhou.

2 May: Ramallah's returnees

Walking up the Jaffa Road to the bus station every morning, I pass a small car rental agency, tucked into the corner of a commercial building. Today, I stopped to talk with the owner of the agency, who had wheeled his office chair out onto the sidewalk and was sitting in the sun carefully paring down the sounding board of what will become a violin. He claims to be the only luthier in Palestine, perhaps in the Arab world—others make many varieties of stringed instruments, ouds and so forth, but he specializes in Western violins. And there's a market for them here: the Barenboim-Said orchestra is based in Ramallah; I've been to string ensemble concerts at the local Friends' Meeting House. A man in his sixties, the luthier had learned his trade from some visiting French instructors at Bir Zeit University, a

few kilometers up the road: he'd been looking for something new to do with his hands, he said; previously, he'd been a chef, but his feet couldn't take all that standing around in the kitchen. Violin-making was easier on them, he went on, then took me into a back office where, in a cramped closet, he had set up his workshop. I learned that he had spent years in Northern New Jersey, but had come back to settle in Ramallah, his hometown, when the Occupation eased its strictures somewhat.

In this respect, he was like a number of other English-speaking Ramallans I've run into here. The owner of a restaurant up the street called Sinatra's (complete with a fedora worked into its neon sign) spent twenty or thirty years in San Francisco; my landlords, as I've mentioned, stayed in Chicago and Gary, Indiana; a café owner had lived in Dearborn, Michigan (along with many other Palestinians), and the man who  will ship my books back to the States next month had a long stay in Alabama, where, he was amused to say, his given name, Kanaan, was turned into "Kenny." The point is not just that Palestinians are diasporic. It's rather that so many of them, after protracted stays abroad, have chosen to return to the West Bank—because they have parents here, no doubt, but also, I gather from these conversations, because this place feels like home.

In 1998, I was being shown around Zagreb by some Croatian academics. Devout nationalists, followers of Tudjman, they were eager to defend their people against the accusation of having participated in the Holocaust, and, more recently, of having carried out a campaign of ethnic cleansing in Bosnia. Walking me past a Zagreb synagogue, our host remarked, in his pretty-good English, "We have many friends here who are Juice." (Yeah, I thought, and who put them through the juicer?) As for ethnic cleansing, they insisted that since Bosnians were Muslims, they were "a nomadic people," and used to moving around (so, presumably, also used to *being* moved around). Like Palestinian Arabs? One of the arguments one hears in Israel against either proposed solution to The Problem—two-state or one-state—is that there are "29 other Arab countries" where Palestinians could happily live among their kind. What this ignores is that—setting aside any religious or ideological commitment to a Homeland on the part of either population—Jews and Arabs alike experience a perfectly ordinary (and honorable) sense of attachment to the places where they have lived. My most radical Israeli friends, dismayed by the direction in which their nation is headed, are nevertheless loath to emigrate— not because they believe this is the Land they were once Promised, but because this is where they grew up.

5 May: vestiges of the Mandate: stone

A medium-sized office building is going up on the Jaffa Road, just behind the HSBC bank. Like practically every structure, old or new, in Palestine, and many in Israel, it will be either built of or clad in Jerusalem stone. I had stopped to watch one of the masons at work earlier in the spring, sitting out of the strong sunlight

and chipping away at each panel to give it the roughened-up look that's considered authentic. Behind him were stacked the hundreds of smooth panels yet to be resurfaced. As the spring went on, I followed the progress of the cladding. The first stone-chipper was joined by another, but that was it: the entire building—several thousand panels, I estimated—would owe the look of its surface to these two men, each working with one mallet and one chisel.

I asked Omar if that was standard practice—was there no machinery that could do that job? He said there were some machines in use in Israel, but that people on both sides of the border preferred the hand-hewn look, and that in Palestine it was always done that way.

Like everything else over here, there's a long history of both practice and ideological investment in practice that explains what I had been observing at this unprepossessing construction site. The practice itself may go back several thousand years; the ideological investment can be dated to the years of the British Mandate, specifically to an edict of Jerusalem's Governor, Ronald Storrs, who had a strong interest in preserving what he considered the city's Biblical traditions and who decreed, in 1918, that all construction should make use of the locally quarried limestone. In a fascinating chapter in *Hollow Land*, the architect Eyal Weizman quotes Storrs's rationale:

Jerusalem is literally a city built upon rock. From that rock, cutting soft but drying hard, has for three thousand years been quarried the clear white stone, weathering blue-grey or amber yellow with time, whose solid walls, barrel vaulting and pointed arches have preserved through the centuries a hallowed and immemorial tradition.

Storrs enlisted the help of the British architect Charles Robert Ashbee, a follower of William Morris's Arts and Crafts movement, to supervise plans for preserving the city's stony heritage. The by-laws they came up with still remain in force, in a modified form, today: when it became too expensive to actually construct buildings of Jerusalem stone, it was stipulated that a thin cladding— what our two masons are working with in the adjacent photographs— should be applied to the structural elements. Weizman describes how, after the so-called "reunification" of the city at the end of the

1967 War, this cladding was intended to confer authenticity on the rapidly added new suburban settlements. Jerusalem stone, according to a citation from the 1968 urban master plan, carries "emotional messages that stimulate other sensations embedded in our collective memory, producing strong associations to the ancient holy city of Jerusalem."

Weizman, who writes with a fine sense of the ironies encountered in such cultural manipulations, goes on to raise the question of just *whose* "collective memory" is being stimulated here: is Jerusalem stone Israeli or Palestinian, originally Jewish or Arab? A great deal of Israeli archaeological energy has gone into "proving" that, "in the beginning" (as Thomas Leitersdorf might have put it) the Arab village was really Jewish. Weizman writes:

> [The] fabric of Palestinian vernacular architecture—found in the hillside villages and Jerusalem neighborhoods—was deemed by Israeli architects to retain not the social-physical typologies that have undergone complex historical development, but fossilized forms of biblical authenticity. Israeli built culture has always been locked between the contradictory desires to either imitate or even inhabit the stereotypical Arab vernacular, and to define itself sharply and contrastingly against it. Zionists saw the Palestinians either as late-comers to the land, devoid of thousand-year-old roots or, paradoxically, as the very custodians of the ancient Hebrew culture and language of this land—all this without any sense of contradiction.

This sort of paradox and contradiction lies at the heart of William Empson's understanding of pastoral, as he laid it out in the early 1930s. He had begun work on

Some Versions of Pastoral soon after completing his *Seven Types of Ambiguity* in 1930, and there is a clear link between his interest in pastoral as a dialectic of opposites resolved or held in suspension and his discussion, in the earlier book, of what he labeled "the seventh type of ambiguity...the most ambiguous that can be conceived, when the two meanings of a word, the two values of the ambiguity, are the two opposite meanings defined by the context, so that the total effect is to show a fundamental division in the writer's mind."

Weizman would locate such a fundamental division in the minds of Israeli architects and, more sweepingly, in the minds of "Zionists." In this account, their imagined relation to Palestinians is bound to exhibit the kind of ambivalence Empson is here describing: the Palestinians are both unlike us, "devoid of thousand-year-old roots," and yet like us, even *more* like us than we are ourselves, in some primal relation to the land.

Such are the perplexities of pastoral thought, a trivial but telling illustration of which may be found in this realtor's sign I came across the other evening in Baka, a lovely, treesy, formerly middle-class Palestinian neighborhood in West  Jerusalem. The key word here is "Arab," an equivocal term that, unpacked, would seem to say: "we have taken back from them what was ours in the first place. This house is valuable because it is 'Arab'— and all the more desirable because you can live in it without having to live with [now, drop the quotation marks] Arabs as neighbors." The sign's being in English, and the Israeli agent's given name, suggest that the targeted buyers are North American, British, or French Jews looking for a *pied-à-terre* in Jerusalem, close to the source. There's a lively market in such confusedly "authentic" properties throughout the city.

9 May: visiting "The City of David"™

Because we are about to devote some classes to the politics of archaeology in Jerusalem, I spent several afternoons this week at what is officially known as the Jerusalem Walls National Park, but most often referred to as "The City of David," an archaeological site, a theme park, and, if truth be told, a public-private joint venture in displacing Palestinians from a neighborhood in East Jerusalem. The neighborhood is known today as Silwan (Biblical Shiloah or Siloam), where Jesus is said to have restored a man's sight. Unlike other Israeli National Parks, the management of The City of David™ has been outsourced to a non-profit called Elad, whose stated aim is to repopulate (with Jews) the area just south of the Old City where, it is believed, King David and King Solomon had their royal quarters. Elad is busy branding the area.

Archaeologists have been working in this neighborhood for over a hundred and fifty years, since long before this Arab village on the slopes of a valley outside the walls had been incorporated into Greater Jerusalem, and they have made some remarkable finds, though perhaps the most remarkable was accidentally discovered around 1880 by a local Sephardi teenager wading through an underground waterway carved out of the bedrock—it has been determined—around 700 B.C.

What he found was an inscription, in early Hebrew, marking the spot where the two groups of miners, one starting to dig from one end, one from the other, had met. It reads:

> "Behold the tunnel! This is the story of its cutting. While the miners swung their picks, one toward the other, and when there remained only 3 cubits to cut, the voices of one calling his fellow was heard—for there was a resonance in the rock coming from both north and south. So the day they broke through the miners struck, one against the other, pick against pick, and the water flowed from the spring toward the pool, 1200 cubits. The height of the rock above the head of the miners was 100 cubits."

You don't have to be a Zionist, or to care much about the accomplishments of King Hezekiah, in whose times this tunnel was dug, to find this thrilling: "a resonance in the rock," indeed! Who knew that ancient miners had such a lyrical relation to their own labor? It reminded me of a time when, biking in Western France, I had stopped off at a village bakery. It was not a shop, just a small working space with ovens in back and, in front, the great metal bowl in which the dough was worked, mounted on a steam-driven vertical axle. While I was there a coal delivery arrived, two men carrying burlap sacks on their shoulders. They dumped them in a bin by the ovens, then stood around waiting to be paid. One of them reached down and idly gave the axle a twist, setting the bowl spinning slowly. "In my capacity as a coal man," he announced, to no one in particular, "*En tant que charbonnier*, I make this bowl turn." A nice bit of French self-consciousness. Even more moving to hear a much more heroic version of the same sort of pride echoing down 2700 years.

The management of The City of David of course is eager to match up stones with Biblical texts, and that is the burden of their brochures and of the signage along the designated itinerary through the site. I came away from that first self-guided tour having seen a lot of stones and been shown, on the accompanying plaques, the apparently relevant passages from the Old Testament. I had read enough to know that some of the interpretations put forward on the plaques were disputed by reputable Israeli archaeologists, and it was hard not to register how tendentious the interpretations were, but that didn't keep the tour, the mere sight of the uncovered stones, the descent into the tunnels, from being fascinating. I decided to come back again, to see what the guided tour was like.

Next day I returned and joined a group that included four Swiss Germans, a couple of elderly American Baptist missionaries who had spent years in Israel working with Palestinian orphans, and another American couple who didn't look either particularly Jewish or particularly Evangelical. Our guide was "Helen," a zaftig, athletic German-Jewish Israeli in her sixties, wearing her honey-colored greying hair long and loose, with a vivid smile and a gift, I was to discover, for offensive humor. We were first led into a small theater, given 3-D glasses to wear, and shown an animated historical reenactment, full of zooming shots and rous-ing crescendos, of the early Israelites, led by David, taking over the very hillside we were standing (or, at the moment, sitting) on, back around 1000 B.C. and turn-ing it into The City of.....David. A foolish film, at once accomplished, in a Disney way, and comically simplistic. It ended with the promise that soon, thanks to The City of David, children would once again play on this hill-side. Of course, children are already playing on this hill-side, they just happen to be Palestinian.

Out in the bright Jerusalem sunlight, blinking after turning in our stereoscopic shades, we listened to Helen's initial orientation. She pointed out Mount Zion, to the northwest, where, in the past, some historians had located David's palace, and the Old City, north of us, where the Muslim holy places, the Dome of the Rock and the Al-Aqsa mosque, now occupied the site of Solomon's Temple. Then she paused, and, with a twinkle in her eye, asked us to take note of the relative positions of the mosque and the Dome: if we could imagine Muslims down on their knees in Al-Aqsa, she went on, directing their prayers towards Mecca, to our southeast, we must see that their raised rear ends would be, of necessity, facing the Dome of the Rock. Helen found this amusing. It wasn't clear whether this was part of The City of David's script, or just a charming riff of her own. She led us over the terrace to look to the east, across the Kidron Valley, to the "Tomb of Pharaoh's Daughter," a small rectangular facade barely discernible among the tightly clustered houses on the steep Silwan hillside, a neighborhood Helen referred to as "this disaster." She went on to explain about the tomb, so named by a 19th-century French archaeologist who imagined that this (eighth-century B.C.) tomb contained the remains of the Egyptian wife Solomon is supposed to have taken in his old

age. Helen quipped that, like many another Jew, he had married out of the faith, a joke apparently lost on the Swiss Germans (who came from a small village near Bern and probably didn't know from *shiksas*). One of the Americans in our group asked about all the litter one could see sliding down among the Silwan houses. Did people just throw their trash downhill? Helen nodded, that's what they're like. But aren't there garbage trucks, regular collections? he pursued. "They stone the trucks," said Helen. The American shook his head, and we left the observation platform to follow Helen down to the first of the excavation sites.

This dissing of Silwan, I knew, was not idiosyncratic to Helen. You hear it all the time from Israelis, even the *bien-pensant* who disapprove of the politics of The City of David. But I was surprised to find it in a recent, finely written and wonderfully informative book by the Cambridge classicist Simon Goldhill, *Jerusalem: City of Longing*. I quote from his chapter "The Oldest City":

> In the Silwan Village on the other side of the valley there is a fascinating necropolis, largely dating from the eighth century B.C., with more than fifty graves in two rows cut into the rock face. Unfortunately, this is not a safe place for Western visitors to go, while the current political situation exists.

(This is, in fact, good advice, but Goldhill goes on):

> Actually, it hasn't been an attractive prospect for a trip for a long while. In 1876 Charles Warren, who went on to fight the Boer and to become the commissioner of police in London when Jack the Ripper was at large, wrote: "The people of Siloam

are a lawless set, credited with being the most unscrupulous ruffians in Palestine." J.L. Porter, the president of Queen's College, Belfast (a tough enough city), ten years later also called them "lawless, fanatical vagabonds," and another Victorian traveler called Kelly, who actually tried to enter a tomb, was terrified by the shriek of an old Arab woman which brought hundreds of swarming children and cursing men and women out of the tombs all around. He fled. Even the modern archaeologist who surveyed the site has little love for it: "Words cannot describe the filth we encountered. At the time there was no proper drains or sewers in the village and the sewage flowed in every direction...Piles of refuse and junk were heaped everywhere." So now it is advisable to see the Tomb of Pharaoh's Daughter from a distance.

My teaching partner, who has architecture degrees from Bucharest and Berlin and a doctorate in city planning from UC Irvine, grew up in Silwan. His parents still live there. His father is a retired school administrator, his mother a retired teacher.

Back to Helen, standing over the excavation of what looks like a very thick wall, with yet another twinkle in her eye. We can't be *a hundred percent sure* this was the site of David's palace, she coyly pronounced, but it just *might* be—the wall is so thick, it had to be a very grand building. The archaeologists are working on it.

That was when I bailed out. I'd had enough of Helen, so, when she headed towards the steps leading down to the famous tunnels, I slipped into a file of Japanese in identical colored hats coming up from below and left The City of David. As I walked back into the Old City, I found my anger growing and spreading: I was angry with myself for not challenging Helen, but more generally and unfocusedly furious, fed up with the lot of them, Jews and Arabs alike, fed up with Palestinian garbage, with being jolted around the West Bank over bad roads in badly sprung minibuses, fed up with the cocky uniformed Israeli soldiers, barely out of their teens, sporting their dark glasses and Uzis on the plaza in front of the Wailing Wall. Even what had once seemed to me the exhilarating diversity (of people, sights and sounds) of the Old City had turned, in this mood, to nothing but jostling crowds, kitsch, and clutter.

I looked around for a calmer, less fraught, place to sit down and cool off and walked toward the north-east corner of the Old City, past the Armenian rug sales-men, to the least dolorous end of the Via Dolorosa, the Pools of Bethesda, where I'd read there was a handsome Romanesque church, St. Anne's. If I'd had it with the bloody-minded Arabs and Jews, perhaps a more famil-iar foreignness might be soothing. I was remembering student biking trips in France to visit Romanesque churches, guided by Henry Adams's *Mont Saint Michel and Chartres*, and one in particular, to see an elegant steeple that Adams was convinced "Jews might kiss and

Infidels adore." And indeed, once through an archway, what I found was very familiar and very French—a small formal garden with careful plantings surrounding a monumental bust that might appear in any town square, depicting in this case not a former mayor or Victor Hugo but a cardinal; and then the church itself, elegantly simple and undecorated, close to some excavations, beds of aromatic herbs, an arbor. The nave was empty, though I'd seen some French priests in white robes as I was coming in. There was a bench in the shade, across from the facade, and I sat down to consult my guidebook. St. Anne's, honoring Mary's mother, was built around 1140, I learned.

Turning back to the page of Jerusalem chronology, I realized that this was not all that long after Godfrey de Bouillon broke through the walls of the city. Here is a contemporary account of that moment in July of 1099:

> Now that our men had possession of the walls and the towers, wonderful sights were to be seen. Some of our men—and this was the more merciful course—cut off the heads of their enemies; others shot them with arrows so that they fell from the towers; others tortured them longer by casting them into the flames. Piles of heads, hands, and feet were to be seen in the streets of the city. It was necessary to pick one's way over the bodies of men and horses. [...] In the Temple and porch of Solomon men rode in blood up to their knees and bridle reins. Indeed it was a just and splendid judgment of God that this place should be filled with the blood of unbelievers.

The entire Muslim population of the city was wiped out, and some indeterminate but large fraction of its Jews. This was not quite what I'd had in mind when I wished myself rid of the bloody-minded Jews and

Arabs. But it was a reminder that there are no untainted spots in this city or this land.

Godfrey's sword hangs in the Church of the Holy Sepulcher, that bewildering structure where, last October, I had heard a weary American tourist ask her husband, "So what woulda happened if they hadna killed Him?" Good question. My Bulgarian-born Jerusalem friend Elizabeth guessed that "there would just have been one more splinter party in the Knesset."

11 May: The City of David™ (cont'd)

On the way to the minimart to pick up some coffee, I pass my landlord's storefront and his father waves me in. He's sitting there with a friend, their hookahs are bubbling away. Old Man Tarifi puts his right hand on his heart: "You are welcome," he says, and with his left hand offers me a round of pita and motions towards the remains of their lunch, there on the table in a shallow aluminum baking dish—a juicy lamb pizza prepared by Nazeeh, the young building manager. His son Khaled comes out of the back office to see if I need anything, then takes off. Our connection is purely business, but no less amicable for that. I've twice lost my house keys, but on the positive side I pay my rent, a hefty $1000 per month, a hundred dollars more than Bard's housing allowance. I'm not complaining; I like the place, and I enjoy, as I wrote in an earlier posting, this Chicago-style family operation. The Tarifis have no interest in politics, or at least they don't let on to me. The night of the Fatah/Hamas accord, a couple of weeks ago, was also the night Barcelona beat Real Madrid. I was awakened around midnight by honking horns and celebratory gunfire. When I asked Khaled's brother, the next morning, which of these events was being celebrated, he laughed: of course it was the football victory—no one cares what Hamas and Fatah are up to. This is not wholly representative of West Bank opinion, but I doubt if it's merely a minority position. On the #18 bus the other day, waiting to be let through the Qalandia checkpoint, I got talking with a Palestinian-American named Mike—another Chicagoan, now running a tow-truck business in Las Vegas. He saw no reason why Israelis and Palestinians shouldn't get along: they're Jews and Arabs, he said, they're not that different; they both like money, they like doing business. It reminded me of a meeting, years ago, in a rundown labyrinthine neighborhood of Shanghai (now probably redeveloped as high-rises) with a local resident who had invited me and my daughter back to his place for lunch, and had quickly whipped up a garlic and noodle dish. Sitting around the low table, he said to Ellen, "Your father looks like a priest." "He's Jewish," she said. His eyes lit up, "Ah," he said admiringly, "the Jews, they are the Chinese of the West"—i.e., diasporic, good businessmen, worldly, more interested in making money than in proving points, etc. In other words, like Mike and the Tarifis.

But, alas, an interest in making money doesn't necessarily preclude a powerful interest in proving points. Elad, the non-profit that runs "The City of David", is dependent on major support from Dr. Irving Moskowitz, a medical man who made his money in casinos and who is committed to reclaiming all of Jerusalem for Jews. Conversely, proving points needn't preclude an interest in making money, and there will be serious money to be made if Silwan's jumble of Palestinian homes ("this disaster," in Helen's phrase) were to be demolished, and developers got to install the sort of upscale residential community that proximity to a pleasantly landscaped national treasure would seem to demand. The City of David is at once a serious archaeological site, a very successful if somewhat hokey tourist "destination" and a developer's dream "community" in the making.

There are several alternative tours of The City of David; I chose one organized by a group of young Israeli archaeologists called Emek Shaveh, having first downloaded their recent booklet, *Archaeology in the shadow of the conflict*, from their website (www.alt-arch.org). The author of that booklet, Yonathan (Yoni) Mizrachi, turned up as our guide last Friday afternoon. There were five of us—a young Jewish couple (he from Philadelphia, she from Venezuela), a longtime American human-rights activist now living in Jerusalem, and a German photojournalist toting the most enviably luscious Leica SLR I've seen outside the B&H catalog. After some preliminary remarks about what we could and couldn't visit—The City of David (being a National Park) is open to the public free of charge, but (because it's privately operated by Elad) you have to buy a ticket for the tunnel walks, and Yoni and his groups are *non grata* at the ticket windows—we went down some steps and stood where Helen had stood our group the other day, looking at the thick walls of what some think was David's palace. "What do you see here?" asked Yoni. "What I see are a lot of stones, which might or might not date from 1000 BC." Archaeological dating is tricky, he went on, stones get displaced, used and reused, and experts agree that there's an odd lack of any evidence that can be securely dated as tenth-century. Clearly there was a sizeable structure here, but what it was cannot, at present, be confidently named as anyone's palace. He discussed the circularity of reasoning—starting with a Biblical text, then digging to prove the text "historical"—that has been the standard procedure of Holy Land archaeology (and has been carefully analyzed in Nadia Abu El-Haj's *Facts on the Ground*). Like Abu El-Haj, Yoni's group is critical of the singlemindedness with which Jerusalem's stones are made to ventriloquize one and only one national/religious narrative. Their own emphasis is populist—not a story of kings and elites, but of all who lived here—multiethnic and multi-theological. Yoni pointed out something that is not mentioned in the Elad literature, the thousands (he emphasized "thousands") of small female figurines found at every Jerusalem dig, fertility goddesses, he believed, that seem to have been worshipped contemporaneously with the Israelites' YHWH.

Emek Shaveh's populism is present-day as well as historical: why shouldn't the (Arab) residents of Silwan, they ask, whose lives are being disrupted by the excavations, be brought into the picture—first, by not suffering displacement as The City of David extends the area of its digs further and further into the village, and second (and ideally) by having their history on the land considered part of the evidence to be unearthed? Although this is the position of a number of Israeli archaeologists [see Raphael Greenberg, "Towards an Inclusive Archaeology: The Case of Silwan/City of David"], there are no signs that this ideal is anywhere close to realization. Quite the contrary. At present there are about 400 settlers in Silwan, inserted here and there in an area that houses 40,000 Palestinians. Elad's current plan is to have another 85 dwellings condemned and demolished so that they can recreate "King Solomon's Garden" in a Silwan neighborhood called El Bustan (in Arabic, "The Garden") east of the current park. Activists have attempted to block this on the grounds that Elad, a private organization, should never have been allowed to operate a National Park in the first place, that it was simply illegal. But last week it was reported that a bill had been introduced in the Knesset that would legalize such outsourcing.

The aim, of course, is not just to make a handsomer and more historically rich archaeological site, but to amp up the pressure on Palestinians to leave the area. The Silwanis know this and, as a result, every Friday, after noon prayers, the youth of El Bustan, the *shabab*, take on the IDF and the Jerusalem police in an exchange of rocks, tear gas and rubber bullets. It was a Friday afternoon, and we were about to take this in, in more ways than one. As we headed along to the next marked site along the excavation trail, we heard shouts from downhill, then gunfire, then smelled the tear gas drifting up the valley. Looking down we could see a file of cops

 heading along El Bustan's main street, then more shouts, running figures, and smoke coming up from burning tires.

Our eyes were beginning to smart: so much for archaeology this afternoon. Yoni led us around to a few more sites of digs, but the rest of the afternoon we spent walking through the Wadi Hilweh neighborhood of Silwan, threading our way among the mixture of Arab

housing and the occasional fenced-in settler compound, sometimes standing aside on the trail so that policemen could trot by us, heading down to the action in the valley. At one point we were standing on a ridge above a house that had been taken over by settlers and could see below us a bunch of kids, settler kids, as curious as we were about what was going on in the streets below. The little girls are trying to look through the gate guarding their enclosure, one brother seems to be boosting himself up to look over the wooden fence, while his younger sibling is practicing his riflery, aiming his green-and-yellow plastic water gun, presumably in anticipation of his obligatory military service, fifteen or so years down the line.

We wound up at the Wadi Hilweh community center, where we sat in a sort of makeshift arbor and listened to a presentation by Ahmad, a man in his thirties, one of the founders of the center. And this turned

out to be an odd experience of a totally unexpected sort. Ahmad seemed to have one leg slightly shorter than the other and limped, but otherwise was a lithe and athletic figure. What he had to relate, illustrated with large color photos, were grim stories of just how nasty the Israeli pressure on Silwan had been—for decades. Indiscriminate arrests and shootings, manhandling of young children, doors broken down in the middle of the night, displacement of families, settlers making themselves at home in formerly Palestinian houses—the now-familiar story of the Occupation, whether one hears it in East Jerusalem or on the West Bank. Ahmad's English was pretty good, but—and this was telling—he was suffering from a really bad case of laryngitis, so his story of oppression came out in a high soprano whine, in some relation to the content of his narrative but totally unrelated to the face and figure of the young man standing in front of us. It was unintentionally comical and became more so when, after some time, the door to the street behind Ahmad opened and a seemingly unending file of grade-school children—twenty or thirty of them—came through, one by one, as he was speaking, pausing to take us all in, then heading for another conference room beyond where we were seated. It was more than distracting and finally Ahmad turned round and—finding his normal voice—said, loud and deep and clear, "*Shabab*, shut up!!" That moment of angry irritation seemed to have done the trick: the rest of his presentation was not high-pitched. Instead, it was dramatically high-tension. Ahmad was telling us of the harassment of children by the IDF while limping over to one side of the room, where he had concealed his crutch, one of the aluminum kind that attaches to one's forearm, the sort you see on people with permanent disabilities. Using the crutch but not mentioning it, he came back to the center of the small room to conclude his talk: he was telling us how he had seen his six-year-old being slapped around by a soldier, had gone to his defense, shouting at the soldier, and had been shot in the leg, in front of his son. Hence the crutch. That was, in effect, the end of the tour. We thanked him, thanked Yoni, who apologized for the necessarily abridged look at the digs, and left.

Backed by the courts and the Knesset, Elad will probably succeed in taking over Silwan. Barring divine intervention, that is—but, if so, through what mediation: Obama? The UN? Another intifada? The reflux of an Israeli strike on Iran? The possibilities seem either unlikely or unthinkable.

Postscript, 14 December 2011: Today's issue of *Ha'aretz* includes a piece on a photojournalism prize awarded for a picture of an Israeli sedan just after it ran into two young Palestinian stone-throwers on the main street of Wadi Hilweh, downhill from Ahmad's community center. It is a dramatic shot: one boy is splayed over the car's hood, the other is caught hanging in the air upside-down, having been projected six feet off the ground. The car's driver, according to *Ha'aretz*, was the chairman of Elad, David Be'eri. He claims he was set up, "ambushed," that the photo was staged, but the photographer, Ilia Yefimovitch (Russian? Israeli? –certainly not

Palestinian) is scornful of this: "Who staged the photo?" he is quoted as asking, "It can also be interpreted in defense of the driver. Who staged it? The children who felt like being run over that day?" The article concludes, "The police later accepted Be'eri's explanation that he was in danger and had no intention of harming the children. The children weren't tried, because they were under the age of 12, the age of criminal responsibility, but a Silwan resident, Mohammad Sharfi who was present, was sentenced to 10 months imprisonment."

15 May: the feud continues

After our Sunday and Tuesday class meetings, Omar and I usually catch lunch on campus, preferably at a spot a couple of levels downhill from the Bard offices, where a café produces a good chicken sandwich served on a crusty baguette. (This is pita country, and crust is hard to come by.) On Sundays, they sometimes feature a special that Omar fancies—a sort of gooey Egyptian noodle and rice dish, comfort food. A sign is taped to one of the pillars on the cafe's porch announcing this addition to the menu. Sitting at a picnic table in a grove of twisty pines we can, if we like, look up from our lunch and follow the line of The Wall separating Abu Dis from Sawahira as it runs down the slope of the road bordering the campus, then up and around a bend leading to the rival village. And so we were sitting there a week ago when we heard a commotion, then watched a file of male students sprinting down the road—chasing? being chased? it wasn't clear, but it soon became clear that the word had gone out to evacuate the campus: Something Had Happened.

People headed for their cars, or for the minibuses, a traffic jam resulted, horns, backing and filling, etc. with explanations being exchanged on the fly. What Had Happened was that the vendetta with Sawahira had been renewed, not on campus or in Abu Dis—where the initial beating and shoot-up had taken place—but in Azaria, closer in to Jerusalem. Still, it was an Abu Dis man who had been gunned down, one of the sixteen who had been jailed for the beating, but who had somehow been freed—as it turned out, all too briefly. "They pumped 40 bullets into him," Salim said, when I spoke to him the next day. I was calling to return his (Sawahira) hospitality and invite him and his wife and kids to a lunch—a lunch for a lunch, as it were—some time before I leave for the States. He had been in touch with his father-in-law, the neighbor of the (original) murdered man. But I thought the payment of blood money had taken care of all that, I said. Well, there was a truce, but the father of the beaten man had vowed to kill six of the sixteen, and this guy was the first of the six to be released from jail. (It later developed that he was the only one of the sixteen who had *not* been in on the beating.) This breaking of the truce, which had been mediated by the Palestinian Authority—it was said that Abbas himself had sent a representative to the talks—must have stung the PA, who may feel they have quite enough on their plate just now: reconciliation talks with Hamas, as well as signs of mounting popular anger focused on the anniversary (today, May 15th) of the Nakba, the enforced Palestinian diaspora of 1948. The next day the papers carried a photo of an extravagant governmental show of force, platoon after platoon of Palestinian police marching down the main street of Azaria.

18 May: the benefactor factor

This morning's *Ha'aretz* (English ed., May 18, 2011) offered the following headlines:

• on the front page:

Watchdog singles out Barak in report on state extravagance, misappropriation

• in its culture section:

**A labor of love or a grave mistake?
The new wing of TAU's school of architecture, designed by benefactor David Azrieli, has unleashed a fire storm**

• and, on an inside page:

Right-wing NGO sues Sheikh Jarrah activists for libel

As you might guess from earlier accounts, I'm most interested in the last of these items, but I think the other two can provide some pertinent context. Everyone here knows *Ha'aretz* as a "left" newspaper with an angle on things, but it's not the *New York Post*, and people take its reportage seriously. This front page article, concerning some fancy dealings on the part of a former Prime Minister, Ehud Barak, the current Defense Minister in the Netanyahu government, is unlikely to surprise Israeli readers. They are used to financial hanky-panky at the highest levels. Currently, another former Prime Minister, Ehud Olmert, is involved in a major real-estate scandal, accused of complicity, when he was Mayor of Jerusalem, with the developers of the visually disastrous project known as "Holyland." There is, as I mentioned in connec-

tion with "The City of David™" and the "Arab" house in Baka, money to be made in providing upscale housing for diaspora families eager to have a place of their own in the Holy City. I doubt if Israeli politicians are any more corrupt than those of other nations. It's just that Israel's a small country and the names of the accused are more familiar.

But big money has another vector, that of generous, outgoing charitable donation, and Jerusalem and Tel Aviv are full of the signs of benefaction. My Hebrew University friends, asked to account for the thoroughly disorienting lay-out of the Mt. Scopus Campus—a series of seemingly endless interconnected spaces rather than stand-alone buildings—joke that it was designed to provide the maximum number of discernible units of space for which individual donors could be thanked. This, too, is not peculiar to Israel: think of all the donated water-fountains, computer terminals, etc. in American hospitals and universities. The Cornell Laboratory of Ornithology even displays a plaque thanking someone for their gift of the seed to be distributed in its outdoor bird-feeding stations.

The Tel Aviv University story is about benefaction as fiasco. It's a full-page spread on the laying of the cornerstone of an addition to TAU's School of Architecture, financed by and—at his insistence—

designed by, an 89-year-old Israeli-Canadian named David Azrieli. Since the school's founding 15 years ago, the article relates, and "in return for naming the school after him, Azrieli undertook to support it by means of a generous annual donation of $300,000 and by paying for a new building if and when the school opens a Master's degree program." That day arrived, and Azrieli proposed, or rather decreed, adding not a new building but a three-story cap of his own invention to the old building, a design the school's faculty considered amateurish but was told it had no say in. Money not only talks, it draws.

All this is prologue to the third of *Ha'aretz*'s stories. Money buys access to power, and it seems it can even buy the right to practice Lone Ranger architecture; the question is, will it also buy justice? You will recall Dr. Irving Moskowitz, the chief benefactor of "The City of David"™, and a prime mover in clearing Arabs out of East Jerusalem. *Ha'aretz* reports that Elad, the NGO that he bankrolls, is suing the Sheikh Jarrah Solidarity Movement for perjury. On what grounds? On the grounds that when Solidarity's activists passed out information recently to tourists near the front gates of the archaeological site, "stressing the damage caused to local Palestinian residents by Elad's operation of the site," they claimed "that a security guard employed by the organization shot dead a Palestinian resident of Silwan." This, said Elad, was libelous: the man was killed *not* by an employee of *Elad*, but rather by someone working for the Housing Ministry. One might ask why a Housing Ministry guard was on duty there, if not to protect Elad's property and the activities it sponsors. It seems that Elad has filed other libel suits in the past year against, in *Ha'aretz*'s words, "a number of activists and leftist groups." In other words, Elad is deploying its considerable financial resources to silence opposition to its activities in Silwan and elsewhere. It's doubtful that any of these "leftist groups" can match those resources, and it remains to be seen whether Elad's money will win the day. And why would Elad choose to invest in this fashion? I suppose one should give them credit for believing what they profess to believe: that all of Jerusalem belongs to the Jews. But, again, were the Arabs cleared out of "that disaster" on the hillside, a nice development—perhaps rather like Holyland?—would look good there. A relatively small investment in lawyers' fees now might produce a splendid payoff down the line.

25 May: Sheikh Jarrah / Shimon HaTzadik

The settlers who are the object of the Friday protests in Sheikh Jarrah would insist that they are not there by chance or through some arbitrary land-grab. Their claim is that the neighborhood is theirs by right—not by right of ancient Biblical history (that too, but one thing at a time!)—but rather of the establishment there in 1876 of a Jewish neighborhood around the tomb of a (3rd- or 4th-century BC) rabbi, Simeon the Righteous. On Israeli maps, the entire section is named for him, not Sheikh Jarrah but Shimon HaTzadik. After our Sunday class last week I asked Omar to drop me off in East Jerusalem—I was on my way to a bookstore on Salah ed Din Street, near Herod's Gate to the Old City—but we got caught in a tangle of traffic right in front of the little park in Sheikh Jarrah where the demonstrators assemble on Fridays. Hundreds of black-clad Haredi were converging on the open area, shepherding their wives and children, pushing strollers, headed into the cleft of the valley, down towards where I'd been told Simeon's tomb was located. I approached an old man to ask what was going on; he walked by me avoiding eye contact. The next person I asked smiled but said he had no English. But I then found a rosy-cheeked man in his fifties with an elegantly dressed wife, an adolescent daughter and a couple of small boys. He turned out to be from Baltimore—Pikesville, as it happened, the center of the largest American Orthodox community outside of Brooklyn. A Hopkins B.A., a J.D. from the University of Maryland, he'd emigrated a few years ago, leaving the law for the Law. He explained that this was a holiday, Lag Ba'Omer, the anniversary of the death of another ancient Rabbi Simeon—Shimon bar Yochai (2nd-century AD)—whose tomb on Mount Meron, in the Upper Galilee, draws hundreds of thousands on this day each year. Because this Simeon had decreed that he should be remembered in joy, not in grieving, my Baltimore friend explained, Lag Ba'Omer is a very happy occasion: "We dance, we light bonfires, we eat a little, we give our three-year-old boys their first haircut... Go over there and see!" He motioned towards the tents that had been set up in the valley. Before we parted, he asked what I was doing here. I said I was teaching Palestinian students at Al-Quds, in Abu Dis. "What are you teaching them?"—I said, "English." "You should teach them power," he counseled. Can I have misheard him? (My hearing isn't all that good.) But if not "power," what word that might have sounded like "power"? I'm at a loss. Was this a subtle Israeli plea for a proper "bargaining partner"? I doubt it. Maybe he said "prayer"?

I headed down the slope toward the crowd coming back from the festivities around the tomb. I heard music coming from a shaded area and started moving towards it, only to be told I was in the women's section—so I was—and that if I wanted to watch the men dancing I would have to go around to the other side. From there I filmed a bit of the dance: men in black forming loose circles with boys in their white shirts, several grandfathers weaving through the crowd with recently-shorn three-year-olds on their shoulders, lots of loud

singing and a clarinet and fiddle playing what my mother used to call "Tzinga-tza-tza!" music. A cheerful and benign scene, in part because of all the children. I started walking away past more families; looking down I saw a little boy in his stroller sucking happily on a pacifier. The rubber nipple was invisible, doing its job in the baby's

mouth, but the rest of the assembly—the plastic disk and its ring—was jet black: it was an ultra-Orthodox pacifier, my first.

I decided to take the long way around to the bookstore and check out the Museum on the Seam, a privately funded exhibit space that displays works with a political or social-protest angle. Its name comes from its location, on the line that, after 1947, separated Jewish from Arab Jerusalem, the "Green Line," so-called because it had been traced with a wide green crayon on a map of the contested city, the width of the mark producing an equivocal no-man's land between the two communities, a sniper's delight in the 1940's and 50's. Once a two-lane road going north through Jerusalem from Bethlehem to Ramallah, it is now a major inner-city highway, six lanes with a median strip on which a light-rail proceeds from Jerusalem out to some settlements. The Cambridge urbanist Wendy Pullan and her colleagues have noted that, while intended to make access to the (Jewish) northern settlements easier, it was later described in terms that attempted to stress its ethnically unifying function— "Peace Way" was one suggested name for it. (Baltimoreans will recall that the major inner ring road separating African-American neighborhoods in the west of the city from the central business district, constructed after the riots triggered by the murder of Martin Luther King, Jr, and serving as a kind of moat around downtown—crossable, but inconveniently so—was, with no ironic intention, named MLK Blvd.) Pullan cites an Israeli planner in 1982 writing of the thoroughfare as a "seam," to be thought of as "sewing together the two parts of Jerusalem into a single urban web." Hence the name of the museum, where, no doubt, the notion of a seam—does it connect? or does it separate?—is likely to be, as they say, "problematized."

I can't be certain of this because the museum just then was closed for several weeks while some new exhibits are installed. I was reading the sign to that effect when an Orthodox family approached, on their way to the celebration, a tall man in his sixties with intense blue eyes, his pale wife, a teen-aged visitor, and his four-year-old boy ("the child of my old age," he later told me, "like Isaac!"). The man (a former New Yorker whose name, it turned out, was indeed Abraham) stopped and asked me, challengingly, "Do you know what this building is?" Without waiting for a reply he went on, "This was the frontier, the front line, the most advanced military post, in the 40s. This building was an old Sephardic residence, taken over recently by some wealthy German and turned into this radical museum which displays the worst sort of left propaganda, the worst of the worst." We talked about Manhattan—he had lived in the East 50s—and about Lakewood, New Jersey, where his visitor was from, a Jewish resort not far from the City, where my grand-mother would take me ("for the healthy air") in the 1930s. I asked him what he did in Israel, and he said "various good works," helping street kids, counseling pregnant girls who were thinking about abortion, etc. When we parted he insisted on giving me his phone number, "in case you're ever in need of help." Looking for some place to write it down, he took out some folded pages and, instead of just tearing off a bit, he handed me the whole works. I glanced at it as I walked along and saw that what he had given me, perhaps intentionally, was the newsletter of a settler group located in Ari'el, the largest religious colony on the West Bank, whose buildings had been pointed out to us, during our walk back in April, on a distant hilltop.

The prose was a nice instance of "right propaganda," though hardly "the worst of the worst." Here's a sampling:

> I believe it is no coincidence that YHVH has placed our diverse little "*Study in the Land*" group in the very centre of the Biblical Heartland of Israel. In fact, Ari'el, the city where we live, is the capital of Samaria, which is located in the centre of the tribal territory of Ephraim, the son of Joseph. This is the very territory which Satan, the archenemy of Israel, wishes to steal from its rightful owners. The Adversary has turned the whole world against those brave and Godly settlers, who are the sole obstacle standing in his way. Consequently, the whole world hates them, as they simply will not play ball and leave the Biblical Heartland of their fathers Abraham, Isaac and Jacob.
>
> This is the reason why we are so happy to stand by these people! In our contacts with the communities of Gilad Farm, Shiloh, Eli, Kedumin, Elon Moreh, Har Bracha, Itamar and Esh Kodesh, to name but a few, all of us in our group have had our eyes opened. In our relationships with them, we have been forced to admit that those people are better than us in every which way! [...] Surrounded as they are by Muslim enemies, who given the opportunity will steal their cattle, burn their crops and kill their families, yet they have such peace and are imbued with a faith to move mountains. On top of this, even their own government will carry out the occasional nighttime pogrom against them by bulldozing their properties. All of this they take in their stride without any rancor or bitterness.

(Only an American could have put together this wonderful mishmash of pseudo-Biblical rhetoric—*the*

Adversary, a faith to move mountains—with colloquialisms like *they simply will not play ball* or *every which way*.)

Yesterday, in Washington, after explaining to our assembled Senators and Congressmen (and -women) that "George Eliot" was really the name of a woman, Benjamin Netanyahu went on to quote her in support of the eternal bond of the People of Israel with the Land of Israel. Commentators were quick to translate "the People of Israel" into "the Prime Minister's base." The newsletter from Ari'el captures the idiom of Netanyahu's base, an idiom he has done his best to keep alive. Infuriating to see it evoking multiple standing ovations from our legislators.

[*Postscript: Later I was to learn that the Museum on the Seam, rather than having been "an old Sephardic residence," as Abraham had claimed, had been designed in 1932 by a well-known Jerusalem Arab architect, Antonio Baramki, and became his family's home. After the 1948 partition, it found itself on the west side of the Green Line, and had then indeed served as an Israeli Army outpost. As for the Baramki family, they scattered into the diaspora; one of them, Gabi Baramki, now a Ramallan, went on to become a Vice-President of Bir Zeit University.*]

30 May: policing in Jerusalem

Two recent headlines in *Ha'aretz* can give you some idea of the current state of public security in Jerusalem. From today's paper (Monday, May 30th):

**Police: Mea She'arim is a no-go
area because of Haredi violence**

The lead paragraph: "Police are reluctant to enter the ultra-Orthodox Jerusalem neighborhood of Mea She'arim because of the residents' violence, a police spokesman said." It seems a man wanted for over a month for his role in what came to be known as the Warsaw Homes Pogrom, "in which a group of Hasidim broke into a home, destroyed the kitchen, poured kerosene over a 1-year-old girl and tried to light the home on fire," is still at large. Why is he at large? "An official" explained that on a previous occasion, when attempting to arrest another member of this group, "we were attacked and the station chief sustained a head injury as a result of a stone thrown at him." *Ha'aretz* included a photo of a stand-off in 2009 as illustrative of what the police were up against. Who are these fearful Haredim? A radical branch of the same anti-Zionist Neturei Karta group I have written about earlier, who deny the legitimacy of the State of Israel, pending the arrival of the Messiah. This particular bunch, *Ha'aretz* reports—on the local principle that there are no current events that may not serve as the occasion for a little history lesson—are "known by some as the Sicarii, after the Jewish zealots who fought the Romans in Jerusalem around the time of the destruction of the Second Temple in 70 C.E." So much for police rules-of-engagement when faced with rock-throwing men in eighteenth-century black hats. Prudent avoidance would seem to have been called for. How about when the demonstrators are non-violent "leftist activists" protesting the establishment of another settlement in East Jerusalem? Another headline, this one from yesterday's *Ha'aretz* (Sunday, May 29th):

Police use tasers against J'lem demonstrators

The regular Friday protest of the group I've written about before, the Solidarity Movement in Sheikh Jarrah, had temporarily shifted to another Palestinian neighborhood, Ras-al-Amud, near the Mount of Olives, where the ubiquitous Irving Moskowitz, M.D. is sponsoring yet another settlement—part of the plan to ring the Old City with a solid Jewish presence or, to put it more in terms of its central intention, to rid Jerusalem of Arabs, to make it impossible for the Palestinians to claim the eastern section as their national capital. As you can see, this is not an occasional building inserted into the fabric of an  Arab neighborhood, but a full-fledged gated community. *Ha'aretz* included a photo of a policeman pressing a stun-gun against the blue-jeaned leg of a young man being held down, curled up, on the road. "I heard one policeman tell another, let him have it a little," said one protestor, "he put the thing to the lower part of my leg. It lasted for four or five seconds. I felt I was being electrocuted. All my muscles were jumping." When I called a friend to find out if he'd been tased, too, he said no, just roughed up a bit. But, he went on, "it was a good demo: I've never seen the police so hysterical faced with non-violent protestors. We're getting to them." If my protestor friends are lucky, the police may wind up as fearful of these "leftists" as they would seem to be of the dreaded Sicarii, right? I would hold off betting on that, pending the arrival of the Messiah.

1 June: Jerusalem Day

June 1st was "Jerusalem Day," an annual cele-bration of what Israelis call the "reunification" of the city at the time of the 1967 War. For many years it involved a parade down Jaffa Street in the center of the city, but lately, under the Netanyahu government, the parade's path has been shifted to pass through Arab neighborhoods in East Jerusalem—another form of making a point. I headed to town hoping to kill two birds with one stone (I realize this is an unfortunate metaphor around here just now): I was planning on picking up some books at the Hebrew University Library on Mount Scopus, then walking downhill to Sheikh Jarrah, to join the counter-demonstration there. The books were for one of our M.A.T. students, novels by the Iraqi Jewish writer Sammir Naqqash (1938-2004), who, after emigrating with his family to Israel in 1951 had refused to abandon his native Baghdad Arabic. I found the books and started downhill, think-ing of what I'd heard recently from Palestinian friends about the emigration of the Iraqi Jews. Rima had told me that many Baghdad Jews had never been Zionists and had been loath to leave, but that the Mossad, she'd read somewhere, had stirred trouble up between them and their Arab neighbors to force their departure. Omar had heard that, too, adding the lurid detail (which he wouldn't vouch for) that the Mossad had strapped grenades to the sides of dogs and sent them into mosques to create havoc and build distrust and hatred between the two communities. Or was it that the dogs were sent into synagogues? I can't remember. And does it matter? The results would have been much the same—if not the results "on the ground" at the time, then the results in the minds and memories of today's Jews and Arabs. This is one of those stories, some true, some dubious, that keep getting told and believed—maybe not even fully believed, but still rehearsed. Like the story, more recent (and, in this case, fully documented in a gruesome video), of the brutal murder of two IDF reservists who had mistakenly strayed into Ramallah in October of 2000, shortly after the start of the Second Intifada.

That story, commonly referred to as the Ramallah Lynching, I was to hear later on my walk that afternoon, in the mouth of a young settler, when I caught up with his group, assembling before the parade, on my way to Sheikh Jarrah. These were a couple of dozen mostly teenagers from Elon Moreh, a well-established religious settlement outside Nablus, not far from (and affiliated with) Itamar. I had seen this young father cradling his two-month-old in a shawl and stopped to ask him about his contingent. I had picked him because he was short and slender and, burdened as he was, seemed unlikely to respond in a brutal (i.e., stereotypically "settler") fashion. This notion of mine about "settlers" was then matched in triteness by this young man's notion of Ramallah: "You live in Ramallah?? It isn't dangerous?? They know you're a Jew??" (I leave you to fill in the rising inflections of disbelief that accompanied these questions.) His English was halting, so he referred me to the group's leader, an older

man named Moshe Katz, originally from Brooklyn and educated, he told me, at SUNY Binghamton. We talked for a few minutes before they all disappeared down some steps into a guarded compound of East Jerusalem settlers, where they would presumably get lunch before they went off to march. The Young Father: "You know Hebrew? You were Bar Mitzvah? You can maybe recite a few lines?" And Katz: "So you're a retired pro-fes-sor! A whatchamacallit... *e-me-ri-tus*, yet!" [*a distant echo of campus idiom drifting in across miles, across years of choices!*] "You're an intellectual! So you should maybe come visit us!" He gave me his cell phone number. I may take him up on it. From a glance at the Elon Moreh website, I can roughly imagine the shape of a visit there, but of course you can never imagine exactly how it would go, what one would see and hear, so I'm tempted and I've been trying his number for the last couple of days, without success.

[*Postscript: I reached Katz a couple of days later and arranged to visit on Monday the 6th, asking if I could bring with me an Egyptian-American colleague, a woman. He said he thought that would be O.K. and would get back to me with directions to the settlement. But I never heard from him again and, after my trip to see settlers-in-action at Hebron, my own eagerness to visit Elon Moreh cooled. Too bad.*]

At Sheikh Jarrah a hundred or so of our Solidarity group had gathered in front of one of several settler houses interspersed among the still largely Palestinian-owned properties, got out the bull horn and started our chants. The occupants of the house responded with blasts of music from speakers they'd set up on the roof along with a large flag and a huge card-board menorah. Soon they were joined by groups of chanting, flag-waving settler youth, coming down from the main parade up the street from us, but accompanied by police who seemed to be intent on keeping order, insisting on some small distance between our group and the settlers. Their youth formed a line, put their arms around their neighbors' shoulders, and started their signature bounce—which at moments looks like a chorus line, at others like a fascist rally. The face-off seemed to have stabilized, not without a few nasty cross-ings of the line. I was impressed with the police and, spotting a tall man who seemed to be in charge I went over to him and complimented him and his men for treating both the settlers and the protestors so even-handedly. Why, I asked, hadn't they done the same the other day at Ras al-Amud, where they had descended on the protest with clubs and tasers? "Oh," he said, "they were break-ing the law that time!"

Never compliment the police: it turns their heads. Shortly after this exchange, the evenhandedness I had been so surprised to observe disappeared. The police line, until now facing outward towards the settlers, keeping them from mobbing the smaller group of protestors, now did an about-face and started herding the Solidarity protesters back from the middle of the street, first back up onto the sidewalk, then down the sidewalk into a tight crowd bumping into another group of settlers. The more the police pushed, the more impossible it was for the protestors to avoid the settlers; the groups clashed, arguing and pushing, until the police moved in and started beating up and arresting....the protesters, of course. I went back to the police commander: "You created this violence!" I said. "I watched you do it! Your men pushed until fights were bound to break out! You did this!" He turned away from me, "I don't understand English," he said. As the arrests were being made, the settler youth cheered; a right-wing parliamentarian in jacket and tie appeared, made a little speech and was hoisted on the kids' shoulders for an uncomfortable moment.

It was time to leave. Another Sheikh Jarrah regular, a German graduate student, joined me in heading for the Old City, where, we knew, the parade was scheduled to end at the Wailing Wall. This so-called Jerusalem Day draws tens of thousands of marchers, but very few of them are Jerusalemites. Most, like the Elon Moreh group, have been bussed in for the day from settlements all over Israel. They poured through the  narrow gates of the Old City, whooping and chanting past the closed Arab shops. We tried keeping up, walking alongside the crowd, but it was a crush and my companion was feeling overwhelmed, dismayed and agoraphobic, so we broke away, cutting through some deserted back streets to cool off. Once beyond the walls, she headed home. I looked downhill towards the plaza outside the Damascus Gate, and was startled to see that it was that spot, even more than the Wailing Wall, that had been the goal of the parade. Its route had been planned, as pure provocation, right through the central shopping district of Arab East

Jerusalem. A float had been driven in and parked across from this landmark building; music blared; crowds cheered. Kids were shouting "Death to the Arabs!" among other chilling slogans. The message was clear—and clearly vectored at the Palestinians: "This city is ours. The whole city. You must go away. Somewhere. We don't care. It's not our concern."

4 June: an integrated economy

This is the envelope in which I was handed a sandwich to-go at Omar's favorite shawarma place, on the main drag of Azaria, up the street from where Lazarus was raised from the dead, down the street from where an Abu Dis man was "descended," as the French say, gunned down in the vendetta with Sawahira I was

following earlier in the spring. The Arabic version of "Bon Appetit!" (literally "Two Healths and Vigor!") is there along with the French, and there's plenty of room above the Arabic for a third "Good Health!" (presumably in Hebrew, judging from the skullcaps on those hungry kids). But it's missing. And my guess is this: the Palestinian shop owner is obliged, for economic reasons, to buy his envelopes from an Israeli supplier. He can't get the supplier's printers to drop the yarmulkes—"It's part of the picture!"—but he can at least get them to run off a few thousand without the Hebrew. Complications of uneven development in an awkwardly integrated economy.

23 June: a context for the vendetta

Soon after one arrives in the West Bank, one learns the special administrative lingo that dates from the 1993/1995 Oslo Accords. Ramallah, for example, (along with other population centers—Nablus, Hebron, et al.) is in "Area A," that is, it is both administratively and militarily controlled by the Palestinian Authority. The largest area—about 60% of the West Bank—is designated "Area C," and is under total Israeli control: it contains most of the settlements as well as great swathes of undeveloped land in the Jordan Valley and the Judean desert. The interestingly equivocal remainder is "Area B," about a quarter of the Occupied Territories, which is nominally under Palestinian administrative control, but Israeli military control. Azaria and Abu Dis, where my campus is located, are in Area B. These designations, according to the *Ha'aretz* columnist Amira Hass, were intended to disappear in

1999, but they remain in force whenever and wherever the IDF wishes them to be in force.

All Area B is off-limits to Israeli citizens, though many of them surreptitiously cross over the line for inexpensive auto repairs and other services. In two recent pieces in *Ha'aretz* (June 19th: "Israel letting chaos rule in Palestinian town near Jerusalem" and June 22nd: "The truth behind another Israeli expulsion trick"), Amira Hass has explored another aspect of the designation of Azaria and Abu Dis as "Area B" by focusing on the context in which the vendetta I've been reporting on took place. You will recall the events: that a dispute over land across from the main gate to the University issued in a brutal beating that sent a Sawahira man first to the hospital, then to his grave; that, in revenge, a café and bookstore on that plaza were torched and the University campus shot up; that a negotiation then took place between the Sawahira family and their Abu Dis counterpart resulting in a blood ransom being paid to the dead man's widow; that a number of Abu Dis men were arrested in connection with the beating; and finally that, soon after being released from prison, one of them was shot and killed on the Jericho Road in Azaria. The root cause of all this violence had been summed up for me by one of the University's security guards as "Ach! Arabs!" That's just (as Helen, the City of David tour guide, might have said) the way they are—tribal, pre-modern: after all, I was told, the Sawahirans are basically Bedouins. Some of our students had other notions—drug deals and disputes over territory may very well have been involved; one, you may recall, even suggested that the Israelis were behind it all, shooting up the campus disguised as "Arabs."

What Amira Hass argues, very persuasively, is that the Israelis are indeed involved in this violence, although not as masked gunmen. Rather, by insisting on the strict limits within which the Palestinian police may operate within Area B—they are, for example, not allowed to wear uniforms or to carry weapons—the IDF has, in effect, turned Abu Dis into a lawless enclave where drug dealers and arms dealers feel free to practice their trades. (This is supported by my students' reports of how easy it is to get drugs there.) What's in it for Israel to promote this situation? Here's what, according to Amira Hass, "many Palestinians have concluded" (I'm quoting from her June 22nd piece):

> Some say the drugs and weapons dealers are collaborators, or potential collaborators, with Israel. This is why the Shin Bet [i.e., the Israeli Security Agency] and IDF are not allowing the Palestinian police to take action against them and why, according to them, Israeli security forces immediately find out about any Palestinian attempt to capture them. Some find here a strategic goal: The worse this intolerable situation gets in neighborhoods that are so close to the annexed Jerusalem, the greater the likelihood that the residents will leave and head over to Area A [for example, Ramallah]. In other words, it's just another expulsion trick.

Amira Hass is careful not to assert this as fact. "Listen to the Palestinians," she adds, "The subjugated excel at analyzing the implications of their rulers' actions. And if the Palestinians are wrong, then why will the IDF not let the Palestinian police operate freely?" Hass's argument here is strengthened by the fact that the men who conducted that hit on the Ramallah Road escaped into

Israel, knowing they wouldn't be pursued there. The Palestinian police had no authority to follow them, and the Israeli police wouldn't be interested in their arrest.

And why should they be? It is a more compelling interest of the State of Israel—or at least of its present government—to promote the stereotype of "the Arab" as irredeemably violent, unreconstructedly "tribal." I've seen how easy it is to buy into this bit of pop ethnography. Amira Hass would demystify her readers of that piquant but vicious illusion.

20 June: a walk in Hebron

In addition to the Byzantine designations of administrative areas I wrote of last time, a further complication is introduced in the divvying up of Hebron, the largest city on the West Bank (pop: 165,000 Palestinians plus approx. 500 Jewish settlers): there is H1 (like Area A, under total Palestinian control) and then, in the center of the Old City, there is H2, where about 30,000 of those Palestinians live along with 85 Jewish families, close to the Cave of the Patriarchs and Matriarchs, where Abraham and Sarah, Isaac and Rebecca, Jacob and Leah, are said to be buried, a site sacred to both religions. Protecting the settlers in H2 seems to require the presence of, I've been told, 1200 IDF soldiers; no equivalent protection, apart from some unarmed Scandinavian "observers," is offered the Palestinian families who find themselves surrounded by both newly constructed settler apartments and former Arab buildings now in the hands of settler families. This has resulted, over the years, in considerable friction and violence. [Anyone with a strong stomach should consult the video put up on line by B'Tselem, an Israeli human rights organization, of a settler mother taunting her Arab counterpart. It can found at: www.btselem.org/video/2008/11/tel-rumeida-hebron].

One leaves the busy, high-rise modern section of Hebron and enters H2 and the Old City by way of a market street. Stretched above the shops are two sorts of screens—bright colored cloths to provide some shade

and, above them, wire mesh and plastic protective sheets covered with litter —old bottles, trash, old dirtied diapers, rocks, anything chuckable—tossed there by settler families living in the apartments above the souk. I had seen similar screens over Palestinian homes in Jerusalem's Old City, strung up there for the same reasons. One senses that the attitude of many settlers towards their Arab neighbors is less one of hatred than of something meaner than hatred: contempt.

I was taking this walk with three of my Bard/Al Quds colleagues, all fluent in Arabic, including one who had made friends with a Palestinian family living in an old building surrounded by new settlement construction. We stopped there first for tea. From their front steps we could look across a narrow alley to a settler's family's clothesline. Things are tight in H2.

Tight in some places and dead in others. Apart from the main shopping street, the IDF has—"for security reasons"—cleared out much of the Old City and welded shut the metal doors to all the ground floor shops, effectively limiting

the local merchants to the one street we'd seen earlier.

As we wandered around this ghost town, we were overtaken by a platoon of new IDF recruits being given a tour of the area by a guide in a red shirt and outback hat. We stopped him and, gesturing towards the emptied streets and the weeds growing out of the old houses, asked how he could justify "doing this to a city—snuffing out its life." He claimed to wish it were otherwise, but said that it was because of the snipers, the Arab snipers, like the one who had shot dead that infant a few years ago. And indeed I had seen the new y e s h i v a dedicated to the

memory of that little girl, just around the corner, near one of the newer settlements, and financed by none other than Dr. Irving Moskowitz. We passed other signs of the settlers' appropriation of structures they had yet to find new uses for, including this mural. The man depicted on the left is Menachem Mendel

 Schneerson, the late Lubavitcher Rebbe, and his image here may be intended as a reminder of the Lubavitcher Hasids long-time relation with Hebron, dating back to 1823.

The Rebbe may be revered, but the more influential rabbinical presence here is that of Dov Lior, Chief Rabbi of Hebron, disciple of Rabbi Zvi Yehuda Kook (of whom I wrote in connection with the Itamar murders) and, as I write, under judicial questioning in Israel for some recent provocative statements he has made. When, in 1994, a zealous American doctor, Baruch Goldstein, machine-gunned down 29 Muslims praying in the Ibrahimi mosque above the Cave of the Patriarchs, it was Lior who proclaimed him "holier than all the martyrs of the Holocaust"; Rabbi Lior is also considered the spiritual guide of the young man who assassinated Yitzhak Rabin in 1995; others have testified to the rabbi's involvement in other plots—fortunately aborted—to blow up Arab buses, killings which he had declared legal in his interpretation of Halachic writings. Earlier this spring he was reported to be worried about the adulteration of the Jewish bloodline by alien sperm. His arrest and questioning last month provoked demonstrations and embarrassed the Netanyahu government, who found themselves in the awkward position of insisting that no one was above the rule of law while saying as little as possible about the content of the Rabbi's preaching.

As we were leaving Hebron's Old City, just around the corner from the Cave of the Patriarchs, we came upon this striking bit of conceptual art. How you read it depends on whom you believe is responsible for it. Architecturally, this window with its ironwork enclosure is clearly part of an Arab structure, but so many such buildings have been taken over by settlers that one can't be sure who's living there now. There was no one around to ask, so your guess is as good as mine: this might be an innocent bit of whimsy, but I doubt it. Or it could be an in-your-face racist taunt on the part of a settler. Such taunting goes on, as I reported earlier when describing the Jerusalem Day celebrations. However, I'd prefer to believe that the Hebron gorilla was installed in its cage by an ironical Palestinian. Take it as a sardonic comment on the racism implicit in The Situation—in H2 in particular and, more generally, in the present Israeli government's dealings with its Arab neighbors.

Or take it as a dark pastoral, the other face of the less tendentious, even rather idyllic image of Ma'ale Adumim on its hilltop with an Arab goatherd and his flock in the foreground.

Afterword (February, 2012)

> As for the nomad Arabs, camel and sheep herds,
> dwellers in black booths and curtains of hair cloth,
> we may see in them that desert life, which was
> followed by their ancestors in the Biblical tents of
> Kedar. While the like phrases of their near-allied and
> not less ancient speech are sounding in our ears, and
> their customs, come down from antiquity, are
> continued before our eyes, we almost feel ourselves
> carried back to the days of the Hebrew Patriarchs.
>
> Charles Montagu Doughty,
> *Travels in Arabia Deserta* (1888)

"Near-allied and not less ancient": Doughty is talking of the kinship of Arabic and Hebrew speech, but the phrase could well apply to the two peoples contending for land and water in this narrow strip of Asia Minor. And Doughty reminds us that, unlike many such contentions, this one is characterized by the imagined likeness of the contesting parties. Suppose that a Jewish homeland had indeed been established in East Africa—a proposal brought to the Zionist conference at Basel in 1903 by the British government—or in Madagascar, an early solution to the "Jewish Problem" considered by Hitler in 1938. European Jews would then certainly have found themselves, as colonists, in conflict with the indigenous peoples, whom they might well have stigmatized as "irrational" and "tribal," but they would not have had to deal with the embarrassing possibility of recognizing themselves in their antagonists, prompting the "paradoxes and contradictions" that Eyal Weizman described in his discussion of vernacular architecture, or the puzzle of who is historically entitled to worship at the Cave of the Patriarchs.

That is what gives the struggle in Palestine its particular "pastoral" inflection. It is true that a quite calculated (highly "rational") appropriation of Palestinian land and water has been successfully conducted over the years and under various administrations by the State of Israel. This has been and continues to be, as the phrase goes, a land-grab, but the motivations behind it are not exhausted by calling it that. On both sides of the frontier, a spectrum of imaginary investments, ranging from theological zeal down through the various intensities of nationalist sentiment, to the more ordinary complacencies of people who just want to live their lives untroubled, has shaped the course of this conflict in ways that have made it seem intractable. Certainly no one I spoke with in either Israel or Palestine expressed much hope for a solution. It is The Situation. One lives with it, although it has been corroding both societies. I've tried to set down in these pages what "living with it" looked like during the winter and spring of 2011 in some corners of Jerusalem and the Occupied Territories.

Suggested reading:

Abourahme, Nasser. "The bantustan sublime: reframing the colonial in Ramallah," *City* 13 no. 4 (2009).

Abu El-Haj, Nadia. *Facts on the Ground: Archaeological Practice and Territorial Self-Fashioning in Israeli Society.* Chicago & London: The University of Chicago Press, 2001.

Agee, James and Walker Evans. *Let Us Now Praise Famous Men.* Boston: Houghton Mifflin, 1960 [1941].

Bachmann, René. *A Wall in Palestine.* Trans. A. Kaiser. New York: Picador, 2006.

Doughty, Charles Montagu. *Travels in Arabia Deserta.* Cambridge: Cambridge University Press, 1923 [1888].

Empson, William. *Seven Types of Ambiguity.* Norfolk, Conn.: New Directions paperback, 1947 [1930].

—. *Some Versions of Pastoral.* Norfolk, Conn.: New Directions paperback, 1960 [1935].

Goldhill, Simon. *Jerusalem: City of Longing.* Cambridge: Harvard University Press, 2008.

Greenberg, Raphael. "Towards an Inclusive Archaeology in Jerusalem: The Case of Silwan/City of David," *Public Archaeology* 8:1 (2009).

Pullan, Wendy, Phillip Misselwitz, Rami Nasrallah, and Haim Yacoci. "Jerusalem's Road 1," *City* 11:2 (2007).

Segal, Rafi and Eyal Weizman eds. *A Civilian Occupation: The Politics of Israeli Architecture*. London: Verso, 2003.

Shehadeh, Raja. *Palestinian Walks: Notes on a Vanishing Landscape*. London: Profile Books, 2008.

Shlaim, Avi. *Israel and Palestine: Reappraisals, Revisions, Refutations*. London & New York: Verso, 2009.

Taraki, Lisa. "Enclave Micropolis: The Paradoxical Case of Ramallah/Al-Bireh," *Journal of Palestine Studies* 37 no. 4 (2008).

Weizman, Eyal. *Hollow Land: Israel's Architecture of Occupation*. London: Verso, 2007.

Photo credits:

Acknowledgments:

I'm grateful to Bard College and to Al-Quds University for having offered me this opportunity, and I'm further indebted to those acquaintances, old and new, Palestinian and Israeli, whose conversation illuminated my stay. In Ramallah, to Mamdouh Aker, Mehrene Larudee, Sophia Stamatopoulou-Robbins, Lisa Taraki, the philosopher who goes by the name of Rima in these pages, and to the couple I've similarly renamed (with perhaps unnecessary discretion) Salim and Rana; in Jerusalem, to Yaron Ezrahi, Elizabeth Freund, Raphi Meron, Tehila Mishor, Anne Nixon, Wendy Pullan, and Liran Razinsky; and at Abu Dis to the devoted faculty of the AQB programs, to our students, and in particular to my teaching partner, Omar Yousef. I'm grateful to a number of others for encouragement or for help with the manuscript and its images: warm thanks to Amanda Anderson, Phyllis Bennis, Louise Bethlehem, Sarah Browning, Sharon Cameron, Charlie Duff, Hent de Vries, Frances Ferguson, David Ferry, Marian Hobson, Ellen Hertz, Louise Hertz, Tom Hertz, Mary Jacobus, Janet Malcolm, Doug Mao, Daniel Murphy, David Rollow, Jacqueline Rose, Jim Siegel, Joy Zarembka, and to the generosity of a donor who would remain anonymous. To Marshall Sahlins and the far-flung Prickly Paradigm Press-people: it's been a pleasure doing business with you.

Some pages have already appeared in the journal *Critical Arts* (26:1, March 2012). I thank the editors for allowing me to reprint them here.

At the blockage of the Jericho Road, in Azaria, looking towards Jerusalem.

Also available from Prickly Paradigm Press:

continued